MW01045831

STUDY OF SLEEP PATTERN AMONG UNIVERSITY STUDENTS

CHINMAY SHAH

Table of Contents

..

List of Abbreviations

AASM	American Academy of Sleep Medicine
AHI	Apnoea Hypopnea Index
AIS	Athens Insomnia Scale
ANOVA	Analysis Of Variance
BHMS	Bachelor of Homeopathy Medical Science
BISQ	Brief Infant Sleep Questionnaire
BMI	Body Mass Index
BPT	Bachelor of Physiotherapy
BQ	Berlin Questionnaire
DAYDYS	Daytime Dysfunction due to sleep
DBAS	Dysfunctional Beliefs and Attitudes about Sleep scale
DISTB	Sleep Disturbance
DURAT	Duration of Sleep
EDS	Excessive Day Time Sleepiness
EDSS/ESS	Epworth Daytime Sleepiness Scale
EEG	Electro Encephalo Gram
EMG	Electro Myo Graphy
EOG	Electro Oculo Gram
GABA	Gamma Amino Butryic Acid
HANDS	Histamine Acetylcholine Norepinephrine Dopamine Serotonin
HSE	Sleep Efficiency
KSD	Karolinska sleep Diary
LATEN	Sleep Latency
LSEQ	Leeds Sleep Evaluation Questionnaire
MEDS	Need Medicines to Sleep
MKBU	Maharaja Krishnakumar Sinhji Bhavnagar University

MSLT	Multiple Sleep Latency Time
NC	Neck Circumference
NIH	National Institute of Health
NREM	Non Rapid Movement
OSA	Obstructive Sleep Apnoea
PQSI	Pittsburgh Quality of Sleep Index
PSG	PolySomnoGraphy
PSQ	Paediatric Sleep Questionnaire
PSQ	Paediatric Sleep Questionnaire
REM	Rapid Eye Movement
RERA	Respiratory Effort Related Arousals
SCN	Supra Chiasmatic Nucleus
SDI	Sleep Disorders Inventory
SDQ	Sleep Disorders Questionnaire
SDSC	Sleep Disturbance Scale for Children
SEI	Sleep Effects Index
SII	Sleep Impairment Scale
SLPQUAL	Overall Sleep Quality
SPAQ	Seasonal Pattern Assessment Questionnaire
SQQ	Sleep Questionnare of Oviedo
STQ	Sleep Timing Questionnaire
SWAI	Sleep Wake Activity Inventory
SWS	Slow Wave Sleep
TST	Total Sleep Time
VPLO	Ventro Pre optic nucleus
WHR	Waist Hip Ratio
WSQ	Wisconsin Sleep Questionnaire

List of Tables and Figures
Tables:

21.	During the past month, how much of a problem has it been for you to keep up enthusiasm to get things done?
22.	During the past month how would you rate your sleep quality overall
23.	PSQIDURAT (Duration of sleep)
24.	PSQIDISTB (Sleep Disturbance)
25.	PSQILATEN (Sleep Latency)
26.	PSQISLPQUAL (Overall Sleep Quality)
27.	PSQIMEDS (Need Medicines To Sleep)
28.	PSQIDAYDYS (Day Dysfunction Due To Sleepiness)
29.	PSQIHSE (Sleep Efficiency)
30.	Overall Sleep Quality based on PSQI Scale
31.	Snoring amongst Participants
32.	Loudness of Snoring
33.	How often do you snore
34.	Has your snoring ever bothered other people
35.	Has anyone noticed that quit breathing during you sleep
36.	How often do you feel tired or fatigued after you sleep
37.	During your waking time do you feel tired fatigued
38.	Have you ever nodded off or fallen asleep while driving a vehicle
39.	Do you have high blood pressure
40.	Berlin Positive
41.	Sleep pattern according to Gender amongst University students
42.	Gender V/S Berlin Questionnaire
43.	Gender V/S Pittsburgh Quality of Sleep Index
44.	Gender V/S Duration of sleep

45.	Gender V/S Sleep Disturbance
46.	Gender V/S Sleep Latency
47.	Gender V/S Pittsburgh Quality of Sleep Index
48.	Gender V/S Sleep Latency
49.	Gender V/S Sleep Efficiency
50.	Gender V/S Day Dysfunction Due To Sleepiness
51.	Stream V/S Epworth Daytime Sleepiness Scale
52.	Stream V/S Berlin Questionnaire
53.	Stream V/S Pittsburgh Quality of Sleep Index
54.	Stream V/S Duration of sleep
55.	Stream V/S Sleep Disturbance
56.	Stream V/S Sleep Latency
57.	Stream V/S Overall Sleep Quality
58.	Stream V/S Need Medicine to Sleep
59.	Stream V/S Day Dysfunction Due To Sleepiness
60.	Stream V/S Sleep Efficiency
61.	BMI V/S Epworth Daytime Sleepiness Scale
62.	BMI V/S Berlin Questionnaire
63.	BMI V/S Pittsburgh Quality of Sleep Index
64.	BMI V/S Sleep Latency
65.	BMI V/s Sleep Efficiency
66.	
67.	
68.	
69.	
70.	
71.	
72.	

FIGURES:

1	Age distribution of participants
2	Distribution of Participants based on stream
3	Distribution of Participants based on stream
4	Distribution of Participants based on BMI
5	Dozing during Sitting and Reading
6	Dozing during watching TV
7	Dozing during Sitting in active in public place,during lecture or at meeting
8	Dozing as a pasagner in a care for an hour without break
9	Dozing during lying down at rest in the afternoon when circumstances permit
10	Dozing Sitting and talking with someone
11	Dozing during sitting after lunch
12	Dozing in a care while stopped for a few minutes in traffic
13	Distribution based on total ESS score
14	Time taken to fall asleep after going in bed (in minute)
15	During the past month how often have you taken medicine prescribed
16	During the past month, how often have you had trouble staying awake while driving, eating meals, or engaging in social activity
17	During the past month, how much of a problem has it been for you to keep up enthusiasm to get things done
18	During the past month how would you rate your sleep quality overall
19	Overall Sleep quality based on Pittsburgh Quality of Sleep IndexSscale
20	Berlin Positive
21	Participants response to Epworth Daytime Sleepiness Scale

Introduction

"Sleep is the golden chain that ties health and our bodies together"–

Thomas Dekker, an Elizabethan novelist[1]

Sleep is a paradoxical element of health. Typically, there is no advice on how to sleep "better." On the rare occasion when doctors address sleep, they might offer, "Get the sleep you need." But how much does an "average adult" need? Six hours? Seven? Ten? Among teenagers, this becomes even more ambiguous. Lay ideas about sleep requirements abound and often conflict with researchers findings that teens should be sleeping more than 9 hours per night[2]. "Be able to wake without an alarm in the morning" is good advice for getting adequate sleep, but this is likely to require going to bed at a time when many other things are happening, including engaging in activities outside the home like sports or other recreation, completing schoolwork, eating dinner, watching TV, communicating with friends or simply talking with your family.

Most adolescents need slightly more than 9 hours of sleep each night, although this varies slightly among individuals. Sufficient sleep is the amount necessary to permit optimal daytime functioning[3].

The two most significant signs that indicate that an adolescent probably had insufficient sleep include the changes in mood and decreased motivation, which often result in emotional and behavioural difficulties. A variety of factors affect the quantity and quality of adolescent's sleep, which include stress, obstructive sleep apnea, caffeine consumption, alcohol consumption, exercise behaviors, jobs, homework, sports, poor time management skills, and school start times. The most obvious factor affecting the quantity of sleep in youths is the time when they go to bed for sleeping and when they arise.[3]

College students tend to sleep typically late at night, and hence, wake up later. Thus, a majority of them manifest symptoms of delayed sleep wake syndrome which is characterized by excessive daytime sleepiness (EDS) leading to poor scholastic performance.

Individuals with delayed sleep wake syndrome wake up late during the weekends[4]. In addition to being burdened by academic workload, young college students are prone to watch television, use computers and smartphones at inappropriate times. The light emitted from these devices inhibits the release of melatonin in the brain, thereby, altering the circadian rhythm[5].

In view of these recent findings, the USA's National Institutes of Health (NIH) recognized adolescents and emerging adults (ages : 12-25 years) as a population which are at a high risk of sleepiness problem. It is based on evidence that the prevalence of problem sleepiness is high and increasing with particularly serious consequences." [6]

At adolescents age, their bedtimes may be delayed, in part, because of a change in their circadian rhythms that regulate their sleep-wake cycle[3]. This shift in the sleep-wake circadian cycle is associated with physical growth changes, cognitive development, and considerable endocrine changes[3]. In addition, shorter sleep time usually results in less energy, resulting in lower interest in exercise and lower calorie expenditures. The tiredness from shorter sleep times might also lead to greater caffeine consumption in an attempt to increase alertness, but many drinks with high caffeine content are high in sugar and calories. These combined physiological and behavioral changes are likely to result in weight gain, which may combine with other sources of stress and complete the shorter sleep duration-Overweight cycle[7,8]. Other disruptions to the sleep environment include activities that may take place in bed such as watching television, eating, working on schoolwork[9], or talking on the phone[10].

College students are noted for obtaining insufficient sleep during the week and for sleeping long hours during the weekend. In fact, students' sleep schedules are so variable that twice as many students as people in the general population report symptoms consistent with delayed sleep phase syndrome.[4,11]

Many students' sleep difficulties extend beyond voluntary schedule variations to frequent, involuntary sleep complaints. At least two thirds of college students report occasional sleep disturbances, and about one third of those report regular, severe seep difficulties.[4,11,12] The problem is even more evident in a recent study that found that only 11% of the students surveyed met the criteria for good sleep quality. The rest of the sample had moderate-to-severe sleep complaints.[13] Students' poor sleep habits may, in fact, be getting worse. One study found that sleep duration decreased from about 7.5 hours per night in 1969 to 6.5 hours per night in 1989[14]

The apparent trend toward self-imposed sleep deprivation, irregular schedules, and poor sleep quality could have far-reaching implications. Poor sleep quality, indicated by subjective sleep ratings, sleep-onset times, sleep duration, sleep difficulties, and daytime functioning, can lead to significantly greater psychosocial distress[15]. Examples include depression, anxiety, reduced physical health,[16] general cognitive difficulties (eg, poor problem solving and attention difficulties[16]), and increased use of drugs and alcohol.[17] Partial sleep deprivation (less than 6 hours of sleep per night) can lead to deficits in attention, concentration, memory, and critical thinking, along with increased depression, irritability, and anxiety.[16,18]. Even students who regularly obtain 8 hours of sleep per night but shift their sleep schedule by more than 2 hours may experience attention, concentration, reasoning, and psychomotor difficulties, as well as increased irritability, anxiety, and depression[19–21].

Unfortunately, students are often unaware of how sleep deprivation influences their cognitive functioning. Pilcher and Walters[16] found that students who stay up all night before examinations that require critical thinking rated their performances better than those students who slept 8 hours, although the all-nighters' performance was actually much worse. The prevalence and implications of sleep difficulties warrant further exploration into underlying factors that contribute to such problems.

A group of researchers[22] who were aware of these concerns investigated the relationship of college students' course schedules, sleep-wake variations, sleep quality, and health status. They found that students with early classes during the week had greater sleep-wake variations than those whose classes were later in the day. Furthermore, the students with more variations in their sleep schedules had shorter sleep duration and greater difficulties in awakening during the week[22]. These findings suggested that inconsistencies between students' social and academic schedules of students may promote variations in sleep schedules and may be a contributing factor to their sleep difficulties.

To date, few anthropological studies have focused on sleep behaviour in general, But sleep pattern of college students in university students in has not been established till date in Gujarat. Thus, Present study was undertaken to find out sleep pattern among university students.

Review of literature

Some of the main questions still explored by sleep researchers today are evolutionary ones, including "Why do we sleep" and "What is the ancestral pattern for human sleep?" Examination of these questions reflects an abiding interest in human behavior and what shapes it, including evolution.

The main functional answer to "why do we sleep" discovered, so far seems to be a connection between sleep and learning, specifically memory consolidation[23,24] where subjects (adults and adolescents) who slept after learning facts or tasks performed were asked to recall those facts or perform those tasks again.

As for the ancestral pattern of sleep, based on both historical documents from the early modern period in Europe and America (1600-1800) (Ekirch, 2005) and late twentieth century lab research (Wehr, 1992), it seems that the sleep pattern may be biphasic. This means that prior to widespread artificial lighting, and in modern times when artificial light is removed experimentally, humans sleep for three to five hours, wake for one to three hours, and then sleep again until dawn. This pattern is by far removed from what we see today, where sleep is typically consolidated into one uninterrupted block.

Anecdotal evidence however suggests that modern sleep patterns vary according to environmental and social variables, with some populations sleeping in a biphasic manner while others sleep in a more consolidated way, often shifting sleep timing to match natural light cycles.

Based on several physiologic parameters sleep can be divided into following two types:

- NREM (Non –REM sleep)
- REM (Rapid Eye Movement Sleep)

Non-REM is divided into four stages (Stage I to Stage IV) based on the pattern of waves in the Electro-Encephalogram (EEG). The EEG waves are characteristically high in amplitude (voltage) and of a lesser frequency (slow waves). As a young adult transits from Stage I to Stage IV sleep, the arousal threshold typically increases. During Non-REM sleep, the skeletal muscles are active, though the person maybe fast asleep. A shorthand definition of Non-REM sleep is that being relatively inactive, yet actively regulating brain in a movable body[25]

REM sleep is so called because it is characterized by rapid, roving eye movements. The presence of these eye movements is used as a marker for REM sleep. Paradoxically, the muscles are hypotonic ; hence, the subject is awake, but cannot move his body. Spinal motor neurons are inhibited by neurons in the brainstem, resulting in atonia of the skeletal muscles. The arousal threshold in

REM sleep is higher compared to Non-REM sleep. A shorthand definition of REM sleep is an active brain in a paralyzed body.

Normal sleep pattern in a young adult

The first sleep cycle : Typically, a young adult enters sleep through Non-REM sleep. After a transition through all the stages of Non-REM sleep, REM sleep follows. The Non-REM and REM sleep is cyclically repeated at an interval of about 90 minutes throughout the night.

When a young adult dozes off, sleep commences with the stage 1 of Non-REM sleep. It lasts for 7-10 minutes only, and is characterized by a very low arousal threshold. Even a minor stimulus such as calling the person's name or touching him lightly can awaken him.

Stage 2 sleep is characterized by appearance of low-voltage waves on the Electro-encephalogram (EEG), called as sleep spindles or K complexes. This stage lasts for 10-25 minutes, and has a higher arousal threshold.

Following stage 2, slow wave sleep (SWS) or deep sleep ensues. Deep sleep is characterized by high voltage, low amplitude EEG waves and include Stage 3 and 4 of Non-REM sleep. Stage 3 lasts for only a few minutes in the first cycle. When >50% of the EEG waves are characteristically high voltage, low amplitude, it is referred to as stage 4 sleep. This stage typically lasts for 20-45 minutes, and has a very high arousal threshold.

NREM-REM cycle : The 'cyclical dance' between NREM and REM sleep continues throughout the night.

In the earlier stages of sleep, NREM sleep predominates. Gradually, stage 3 and 4 of Non-REM sleep are replaced by stage 2 sleep; REM sleep also becomes longer. Non-REM sleep and REM sleep alternate throughout the night at an interval of 90-110 minutes.

Distribution of sleep stages throughout the night: In a young adult, slow wave sleep (SWS) dominates in the first third of the night; while, in the latter third REM sleep occurs predominantly. This pattern is driven by the homeostatic drive and circadian drive respectively [Oscillation of the body temperature is an index of regulation by a circadian mechanism].

Regulation of the sleep-wake cycle: For a proper understanding of sleep, it is essential to understand the mechanism of wakefulness. The reticular activating system in the brainstem releases the famous five- neurotransmitters that promote wakefulness. These are histamine, acetylcholine, nor-epinephrine, dopamine and serotonin (mnemonic- HANDS). Integrity of the brainstem reticular activating system is essential for wakefulness.

The sleep/wake switch : The sleep/wake switch is the link between wakefulness and sleep. It consists of two sets of neurons in the hypothalamus : neurons that promote wakefulness and those that herald the onset of sleep. Wake promoter neurons are located in the tubero-mamillary nucleus of the hypothalamus. They release the neurotransmitter histamine. Sleep promoting neurons are located in the Ventro-lateral pre-optic nucleus (VLPO) of the hypothalamus. They release the neurotransmitter Gamma=Amino Butyric Acid (GABA). In addition, two other sets of neurons play an equally important role. They are orexin containing neurons in the lateral hypothalamus and the supra-chiasmatic nucleus (SCN), which releases the hormone melatonin.

Sleep is critically dependent on the 'circadian drive' and the 'homeostatic drive'. The circadian rhythm is dependent on clues in the environment called as 'zeitgebers.' It causes the release of the hormone melatonin from the Suprachiasmatic Nucleus (SCN) of the hypothalamus. Thus, torchbearer of the circadian drive is the hormone melatonin, while adenosine is the one that controls the homeostatic drive. As the circadian drive wanes, and the homeostatic drive sets in : (a) melatonin is released (b) the tubero-mamillary nucleus is turned off and (c) the ventro-lateral pre-optic nucleus is turned on. The VLPO releases the neurotransmitter GABA which heralds sleep.

Adequate amount of sleep is important for one's mental and physical health, for cognitive restitution, processing, learning and memory consolidation[26,27]. Sleep requirements vary from person to person but 7-8 hours of sleep in adults is considered normal. A good quality of sleep is essential to enable university students to comprehend, analyse, and absorb enormous amounts of information during the study process, yet they commonly endure sleep problems[28]. In a survey conducted on 1462 university students, 1038 (71%) expressed dissatisfaction with their sleep[14]. Inadequate duration as well as poor quality of sleep negatively affect their concentration, leading to tardiness or even absence from classes.

" Sleep is a criminal waste of time and a heritage from our cave days." –

Thomas Edison[1]

Thomas Edison's heartfelt words epitomize the view about sleep harboured by most university students. Adolescence and young adulthood is a pivotal stage in life. The young adult's prefrontal cortex has not reached full maturation. Hence, this stage is vulnerable to the deleterious effects of stress. Sleep deprivation is one such sort of trigger, which can alter the homoehstatic response. Significant developmental milestones have to be attained in adolescence and young adulthood. These include completion of high school and choosing a career, completing university education with reasonable scholastic achievement and forming mature adult relationships. This makes the adolescent vulnerable to the deleterious to the harmful effects of sleep deprivation (Louca et al, 2014).

The consequences of sleep problems, whether due to insufficient sleep or an untreated sleep disorder can be serious. Sleep problems have been associated with deficits in attention and[29,30] academic performance , drowsy driving , risk taking behavior[31] , impaired relationships[32] , and[33] poor health . Excessive daytime sleepiness due to sleep deficiency was associated with increased risks for accidents, decreased productivity and difficulties in interpersonal relationships[34] . It was reported that insomnia caused problems such as impaired concentration, impaired memory and decreased ability to accomplish daily tasks[35] .

University students have been exposed to a lot of pressure due to academic demands. Moreover, the sleep-wake cycle of the students is characterized by insufficient sleep duration, delayed sleep onset and occurrence of napping episodes during the day.

Over a decade, craze of audio and video gadgets and late night video-gaming zones among people and especially among students has increased. Development of these new media has been changing culture and lifestyles of young adults including university students. Due to these lifestyle changes, sleep patterns of young adults tend to become irregular and many of them experience sleep deficiency, which could have detrimental effects on daytime activities including study[36] . The purpose of the present study was to determine the prevalence of sleep tried to correlate with Gender, BMI and stream they are studying in.

There have been various reasons for decreased sleep in adolescents including watching TV and using the internet[37]. A study done in a Pakistani medical university showed that 58.9 percent of the adolescents slept less than 8 hours a day and the most common cause of sleep deprivation was watching television and listening to music. Stress, in adolescents, is also a very important contributing factor in inability to sleep at night[5].

Another trend seen among students is consumption of caffeine, pain killers, substance abuse and smoking at night to keep them awake. This greatly contributes to sleeplessness at night among students and affects their academic performances adversely. The College students are at a greater risk of developing sleeping disorders and this can adversely affect their academic performance[38]. A study carried out in University of Colorado School of medicine suggested that sleep disturbances negatively affect student performances at different ages and educational levels15. A similar study done in China demonstrated that a large number of college students had sleeping difficulties[16].

It is believed that disturbances in sleep are associated with poor social performance and various somatic and psychiatric disorders[39-41]. Sleep disorders among university full-time students who are experiencing high levels of stress because of the demands of academic performance is an important topic for investigation[42-44]. However, little research has focused on this group of individuals. Most studies have focused instead on young children, older adults or on a certain category of patients[45-47] Today's university students experience great psychological pressure due to the changing career options and increased competition for jobs[48].

Various researches have been conducted all over the word on this issue so far which shows that sleep deprivation affects the academic performance of student and may also cause mood dysregulation, increased dissatisfaction in day time functioning, obesity and decrease in cognitive functions. The study of sleep should not only refer to the fact of sleeping well at night but also should include the examination of daytime functioning[49]

A total of 13 % of adolescent have sleeping difficulties during the night, 10 % report difficulties to get to asleep[50] and there is greater association with psychiatric disorders such as anxiety, depression, attention deficit and behavioural disorders in those who have problems during sleep as well as being prone to accidents and day time hypersomnia[51]. Those people with suicidal tendencies have higher rate of alterations in quality, latency and duration of sleep in comparison with normal[52]. We can summarise consequences of inadequate Sleep in Table below:

Table No 1: consequences of inadequate Sleep

Short Term Consequences	Long Term Sequences
Higher Depression, Anxiety, Lower Self Esteem	Psychological problems, especially more anxiety, depression
Links to Substance Abuse	Potential for increased BMI
Poorer Self-Regulation and impulse control	Potential for re wired brains/ prefrontal cortex effects
Poorer memory for new tasks or information, poorer performance on tasks, poorer grades	Setting up poor sleep patterns for the future
Increased chance of getting sick	
Injury or death from drowsy driving/ falling asleep at the wheel	

Sleep duration makes up one third of our life. It has been established that there is a 35 % prevalence of sleep alterations at some time in life in the general population[53].

A total of 13 % of adolescent have sleeping difficulties during the night, 10 % report difficulties to get to asleep[54] and there is greater association with psychiatric disorders such as anxiety, depression, attention deficit and behavioural disorders in those who have problems during sleep as well as being prone to accidents and day time hypersomnia[51].

Given that the impact that sleep has on mental health and that it is difficult to make adequately define and quantify it, instruments are needed for its evaluation and measurement that can decrease the bias due to subjectivity. Some existing scales require the person to answer retrospectively according to what he/she recalls of his/her quality of sleep during the last month[55].

All the knowledge on sleep has been applied to the development of scales designed to evaluate sleep characteristics and disorders in the child, adolescent and adult population.

Sleep evaluation scales and questionnaires: The scales used to evaluate the characteristics of cognitive and behavioral functioning of persons and make it possible to obtain data that orient towards the diagnoses, especially in the area of mental health and neurology. Many scales have been developed in different health care field settings. These scales measure the altered states of behaviour as well as the personality disorders, and emotional states[56].

When the scale is elaborated or translated from another language, it should be validated and the reliability of the instrument should be established for populations where it is going to be used. Different statistical techniques can be used to determine instrument reliability. One of these uses point dispersion and is calculated with the variance between the points expected in those obtained. The greater the level of reliability, the lower the measurement error[53].

A valid instrument is that which really measures the quality or characteristics for which it has been designed. There are different types of validation tests, that is, predictive content and construct. The concept of sleep quality is a construct that may be evaluated using self-report scales. The resulting elements vary according to the individuals surveyed. This type of evaluation is basically subjective and includes quantitative aspects such as sleep duration, number of awakenings, latency time, and qualitative aspects such as sensation of rest, mood state or oneiric content[53].

The study of sleep should not only refer to the fact of sleeping well at night but also should include the examination of daytime functioning[57]. The subjective report of the patient is of great importance in sleep alterations, for example, the definition of insomnia includes subjective malaise associated with the onset or maintenance of sleep, however the opinions vary according to the individuals[58].

SCALES THAT EVALUATE SLEEP AND OTHER PARAMETERS

Scale for the Infant Population (Table-2) :

- The short questionnaire on sleep in infants, Brief Infant Sleep Questionnaire (BISQ), is an instrument designed for the pediatric population[59].

- The Sleep Disturbance Scale for Children (SDSC)[60] is made up of 27 Likert type items and is designed to detect sleep analysis

- Another sleep evaluation scale in children and adolescents is the Pediatric Sleep Questionnaire (PSQ)[61]. This evaluate 22 items and its accuracy, reliability and sensitivity is greater than 0.80. This instrument is characterized by the fact that it compares sleep disorders and daytime sleepiness with lack of attention and hyperactivity symptoms and also correlates them with the findings of polysomnography.

Table No 2: Scale to evaluate sleep in Child Population

Instrument	Origin site	References	Aspects evaluated	Period evaluated
Brief Infant Sleep Questionary (BISQ)	Tel Aviv (Israel)	Sadeh. Pediatrics, 2004	Hour of sleeping, duration of sleep (night-day), nighttime wakings	Sleep in last week
Sleep Disturbance Scale for Children (SDSC)*	Roma (Italia)	Bruni O. J Sleep Res, 1996	Sleep disorder (26 items)	Retrospective up to 6 months
Pediatric Sleep Questionnaire (PSQ)	Michigan (USA.)	Chervin RD. Sleep Med, 2000	Snoring, daytime sleepiness and inattentive-hyperactive behavior (22 items)	Night prior to polysomnography

* Includes adolescent population.

Scales for the adolescent population(Table-3):

Many scales or questionnaires to evaluate sleep in adolescents were found in the bibliography reviewed. Although most have been developed recently, among these three have existed for more than 20 years.

Table No 3: Scale to evaluate sleep in Adolescent Population

Instrument	Origin site	References	Aspects evaluated	Period evaluated
Sleep Impairment Index (SII)	USA	Smith S. J Sleep Res, 2001. Morin, 1993	Sleep perception in relationship with daytime occupation	Daily for 2 weeks
Sleep-Wake Activity Inventory (SWAI)	Unknown	Smith S. J Sleep Res, 2001. Rosenthal, 1993	Sleepiness (59 items)	Daily for 2 weeks
Sleep Disorders Questionnaire (SDQ	Unknown	Smith S. J Sleep Res, 2001. Douglass, 1994	Physiological sleep and disorders (176 items)	Daily for 2 weeks
Dysfunctional Beliefs and Attitudes about Sleep Scale (DBAS)*	Unknown	Smith S. J Sleep Res, 2001. Morin,1993	Perception and beliefs on the sleep alterations (insomnia) (30 items)	Daily for 2 weeks
School Sleep Habits Survey (modified)	Rhode Island (USA)	Giannotti. J Sleep Res, 2002	Sleep habits, daytime sleepiness, school attendance, chronotypes, emotional aspects and substance consumption	Last 2 weeks
Sleep survey for adolescents	Island	Thorleifdottir B. J Psychosomatic Research, 2002	Sleep, sleep habits and sleep problems	Daily (in the morning) for 1 week)
Post-Sleep Inventory*	Unknown	Webb WB. Percept Mot Skills, 1976	Pre, during and post-sleep aspects (mental activity, sleep factors, good and bad sleep) (29 items)	Evaluation of a single night
Sleep Questionnaire*	Unknown	Johns MW. Br J Prev Soc Med, 1971	Latency, time of getting up, total sleep time, sleep quality (27-31 items)	Previous night
Post-Sleep Questionnaire (PSQ)/Sleep Effects Index (SEI)*	Unknown	Zammit GK. J Clin Psychol, 1988	Latency, total time, maintenance, dysphoria, sleepiness, motor involvement, social (28 items)	

* Includes adult population.

- The Sleep Impairment Index[62,63] (SII) scale evaluates sleep perception in relationship with daytime occupation. It includes five items which describes the severity of the disorder viz the onset of sleep, sleep maintenance and waking problems in the morning as well as interference of daytime functioning and dissatisfaction grade with the current sleep pattern.

- The Sleep-Wake Activity Inventory[64] (SWAI) is a self-report one with 59 items designed specifically to identify excessive daytime sleepiness, but includes five additional factors: nighttime sleep, energy level, discomfort, desire to socialize and ability to relax. Some of these items are relevant to evaluate other aspects that may be related with insomnia, especially those regarding energy level and desire to socialize.

Scale to evaluate sleep in Adult Population (Table 4):

- The Sleep Disorders Questionnaire[65] (SDQ) is a questionnaire having 176 items designed to evaluate the presence of common sleep disorders. It includes four main factors: sleep apnea, narcolepsy, psychiatric sleep problems and periodic limb movement disorder. The authors state that the questionnaire is designed more to give any diagnosis than for a description of the disorders.

- Morin published the Dysfunctional Beliefs and Attitudes about Sleep Scale [66](DBAS) to identify specific, irrational and affect-loaded thoughts that hinder sleep onset. This includes 30 items organized into 5 subscales: erroneous concepts on the causes of insomnia, erroneous attributions or «amplifications» of the consequences of insomnia, unrealistic expectations on sleep, perception of lack of control and defective beliefs on the practices the promote sleep

- Other instruments that evaluate sleep in adolescents are the School Sleep Habits Survey[67], sleep survey for adolescents in Iceland[68],

Table No 4: Scale to evaluate sleep in Adult Population

Instrument	Origin site	References	Aspects evaluated	Period evaluated
Oviedo Sleep Questionnaire (OSQ)	Oviedo (Spain)	Bobes, 1988. Bobes, 2000	Sleep times and sleep perception (15 items)	Last month
Sleep Timing Questionnaire (STQ)	Pittsburgh (USA)	Monk J. Sleep Res, 2001	Sleep times (going to bed, waking up, and ideal sleep times	Daily for two weeks
Sleep Disorders Questionaire (SDQ)	Unknown	Douglas A. Sleep Res, 1986	Sleep disorders (165 items)	
Sleep Disorders Questionaire (SDQ)	Unknown	Sweere Y. J Psychosomatic Research, 1998	Physiological sleep, depression, insomnia, narcolepsy and apnea (34 items)	Daily for two weeks
Wisconsin Sleep Questionnaire. Validación en Francia	Wisconsin	Teculescu D. J Clin Epidemiol, 2003. Young, 1993	32-10 (sleep disorders due to breathing), 5 (sleep disorder), 5 (personal), 12 (habits and work)	Retrospective (week) and follow-up at 3 months
Sleep Disorders Inventory (SDI)	USA	Tractenberg RE. J Sleep Res, 2003	Alterations in sleep (8 items)	Retrospective 2 weeks
Pittsburgh Sleep Quality Index (PSQI)*	USA	Buysse DJ. Psychiatry Res, 1989	Sleep disorders (19 personal items + 5 items answered by partner or caregiver)	Interval of 1 to 12 months
Leeds Sleep Evaluation Questionnaire (LSEQ)	Leeds (England)	Zisapel N. J Sleep Res, 2003	Sleep quality	During 7 weeks (evaluates 1 night of sleep
Sleep Disturbance Questionnaire (SDQ)		Espie CA. J Behav Ther Exper Psychiatry, 1989	Insomnia (12 items)	
VSH Sleep Scale	Unknown	Snyder-Halpern R, Verran JA. Res Nurs Health, 1987	8 characteristics of sleep, fragmentation, duratino, latency, deepness	
Basic Nordic Sleep Questionnaire (BNSQ)	Unknown	Partinen M. J Sleep Res, 1995	Quantitative and qualitative aspects of sleep (26 items)	
Sleep Evaluation Questionnaire	Unknown	Parrot AC. Psychol Med, 1978	Tme of going to bed, quality of sleep, time of waking up, behavior on getting up (10 items)	Evaluation of a single night
Karolinska Sleep Diary (KSD)	Sweden	Akerstedt T. Percept Mot Skills, 1994	Sleep quality, latency, ease of waking up, continuity (12 items)	Evaluation of a single night
Lindberg	Sweden	Lindberg E. J Sleep Res, 2000	Sleep alteration and symptoms (71 items)	Dialy
Athens Insomnia Scale (AIS)	Athens (Greece)	Soldatos CR. J Psychosom Res, 2000	It quantifies difficulty in sleep (onset, wakings, duration, quality) according to ICD-10 criteria (8 items)	Retrospective (last month)
Sleep Problems Scale	Boston (USA)	Jenkins CD. J Clin Epidemiol, 1988	Sleep disorders (3 and 4 items)	Self-evaluation (registries of 1 month-6 months?)
Disfunctional Beliefs and Attitudes about Sleep Scale-10 (DBAS-10)*	Glasgow (Scotland)	Espie CA. J Psychosomatic Research, 2000	Long and short term beliefs on insomnia and its control (10 items)	Daily for two weeks
Epworth Sleepiness Scale (ESS)*	Melbourne (Australia)	Johns MW. Sleep, 1991. Gibson ES. BMC Public Health, 2006	Sleepiness (9 items)	Immediate
Visual Analog Scale in quality of sleep (VAS-QOS)	Tel Aviv (Israel)	J Sleep Res, 2003	Sleep perception (insomnia)	During 7 weeks
Calgari Sleep Apnea Quality of Life Index (SAQLI)	Calgary (Canada)	Am J Respir Crit Care Med, 1998	Sleep apnea (daily, social, emotional function, symptoms and therapy) (35 items)	Immediate (4 weeks after treatment)
Sleep-EVAL system	Unknown	Ohayon M. J Sleep Res, 2002	Insomnia	Immediate (by telephone)
St. Mary's Hospital Sleep Questionnaire	Unknown	Ellis BW. Sleep, 1981	Sleep quality, latency, continuity, satisfaction (14 items)	Evaluation of a single night

St. Mary's Hospital Sleep Questionnaire	Unknown	Leigh TJ. Sleep, 1988	Sleep quality, latency, continuity, satisfaction (14 items)	Evaluation of a single night
Sleep Questionnaire	Unknown	Domino G. Percept Mot Skills, 1984	Difficulty to wake up, Quality (latency), duration, irregularities, negative affect, recall (55 items)	
Stanford Sleepiness Scale (SSS)*	Stanford (USA)	Hoddes E. Psychophysiology, 1973	Evaluation of sleepiness on 7 levels	Every 15 minutes or at any time
Subjective assessment scale of sleep and dreams	Mexico	Gruen, Martinez, Cruz-Ulloa, Aranday, Calvo. Salud Mental, 1997	Emotional aspects of sleep and dreams	The night before

* Includes adolescent population.

post-sleep inventory[69], Sleep Questionnaire[70] and Post-Sleep Questionnaire/Sleep Effects Index (PSQ/SEI)[71].

- Giannotti et al[67] from the Sleep Study Center of the University La Sapienza in Rome slightly modified and validated in Italy the original School Sleep Habits Survey of Carskadon et al[72,73]. The final instrument evaluated sleep, sleepiness, substance use, anxiety, depressive mood, use of sleeping pills, school attendance and circadian preferences (morninguess-eveninguess) of the adolescents during the last two weeks of its application and this is made up of several subscales that measure these aspects.

- Scales that evaluate sleep times on physiological sleep, sleep disorders in general, insomnia, sleep quality, sleep apnea and sleepiness. Included among the tests related with sleep time in physiological sleep are the Sleep Quality Questionnaire of Oviedo (SQQ), Sleep Timing Questionnaire (STQ), VSH Sleep Scale of Snyder-Halpem, elaborated around the year 1987, Basic Nordic Sleep Questionnaire of Partinen of

1995, Sleep Evaluation Questionnaire[74] and Karolinska Sleep Diary (KSD)[75].

- There are many tests that evaluate sleep disorders in general, among them the Sleep Disorders Questionnaire (SDQ), Wisconsin Sleep Questionnaire (WSQ), developed by Lindberg et al[76], Sleep Disorders Inventory (SDI), Pittsburgh Sleep Quality Index (PSQI), the Athens Insomnia Scale (AIS) instrument[77] and the Sleep Problems Scale[78]. The Sleep Disorders Questionnaire (SDQ) was designed by Douglas et al[79] and then modified and validated in Holland36. These questionnaires aim to evaluate common sleep disorders. The original one had 165 items and the Dutch version reduced this to 34 items. These questionnaires evaluate in physiological sleep, depression, insomnia, narcolepsy and sleep apnea. The Wisconsin Sleep Questionnaire (WSQ) is a short instrument designed to investigate sleep problems such as snoring, apnea and others such as difficulties of getting to sleep, getting out of bed at night or too early, sensation of not having rested, waking difficulty, nightmares, daytime sleepiness, restlessness and going to sleep, nasal obstruction or drip and falling asleep while watching television or reading. It showed a significant internal consistency (Cron-bach's alpha: 0.67-0.81) and maintained its validity in the measurements made at an interval of 3 months (Cohen's kappa > 0.60). Among these, the Seasonal Pattern

Assessment Questionnaire (SPAQ)[80] is included. Among other things, this evaluates the effects of the seasonal changes on sleep.

- However, the Leeds Sleep Evaluation Questionnaire[81] (LSEQ) is a standardized instrument to measure difficulties to sleep in the context of clinical investigation. It is a retrospective instrument in which the patients are asked to compare current aspects of sleep with those prior to the study they are enrolled in. It is made up of ten 10 cm line visual analogue scales to evaluate four domains (getting to sleep, sleep quality, waking and behavior after waking). The LSEQ is applied repetitively and the difference between current measurements and previous ones is used to evaluate efficacy of the study drug.

- Epworth Daytime Sleepiness Scale (EDSS)[82]: It is a scale intended to measure daytime sleepiness that is measured by use of a very short questionnaire. This can be helpful in diagnosing sleep disorders. It was introduced in 1991 by Dr. Murray Johns of Epworth Hospital in Melbourne, Australia. The questionnaire asks the subject to rate his or her probability of falling asleep on a scale of increasing probability from 0 to 3 for eight different situations. The scores for the eight questions are added together to obtain a single number. A number in the 0-9 range is considered to be normal while the numbers 10 and 11 are border line and 12-24 range indicates that expert medical advice should be sought.

- Pittsburg Quality of Sleep Index (PQSI)[83]: It is a self report instrument designed to assess sleep quality during the past month and contains 19 self-rated questions from which 7 component scores are calculated and summed into a global score.1 Higher scores represent worse sleep quality: component scores range from 0 to 3, and global scores range from 0 to 21. It analyze factors such as sleep quality, sleep latency, sleep duration, sleep efficiency, sleep disturbance and use of sleep medication.

- This Index is an internationally recognised instrument used to evaluate sleep behaviours in the preceding month[84].8 It entails 19 items and has a reliability coefficient (Cronbach's alpha) of 0.83 for its seven components.9 Numerous studies using the PSQI have supported its high validity and reliability.10-12 The total PSQI score ranges from 0 to 21; higher scores reflect poorer quality of sleep. In general, a PSQI score of higher than 5 is considered to indicate poor sleep quality[15,84].

- Berlin Questionnaire (BQ)[85]: The BQ is a screening tool used widely for the identification of Subject who may be at high risk for OSA. Subjects can be divided in high risk and low risk of OSA based on responses to symptom questions grouped in three categories. They will be considered to be at high risk for sleep apnea if 2 of the 3 following criteria were met: 1) snoring with two of the following features: louder than talking, at least 3 to 4 times a week, complaints by others about snoring, witnessed breathing pauses at least 3 to 4 times a week; 2) early morning and daytime fatigue exceeding 3 to 4 times a week or having fallen asleep while driving; and 3) presence of hypertension or obesity.

Most of the sleep scales reviewed aim to evaluate the alterations and diseases present in both the general as well as specific populations (elderly, children, adolescents, dementia patients and those with other diseases). In these scales, there are often questions on the characteristics of sleep that have occurred in periods distant from the time when the questionnaire is applied.

As Lund et al point out, few carefully designed studies have captured and articulated college-age adolescents or emerging adults' changing sleep patterns[86]. After age 20, Roenneberg et al found that the mid-point times became increasingly earlier again[87]. Although this is cross sectional data, it suggests that the timing of sleep changes over the course of emerging adulthood.

A small number of studies have examined sleep/wake patterns over the transition from high school to college. In a brief report, Carskadon and Davis surveyed close to 1000 undergraduate students in the spring before entering college, and again during the first fall semester[73]. These preliminary findings showed a significant pattern of sleeping less and delaying nighttime sleep by about 2 hours across the transition to college.

Pilcher et al documented that sleep habits are one of the first daily habits to change for first-year college students, and other studies found that college students, in general, exhibit irregular sleep-wake cycles with bedtime delays on weekends and short sleep durations on weekdays88–91. Moreover, college students today are getting less sleep than students in the past, and a high proportion of students suffer from a number of sleep problems. National surveys of undergraduates, for example, have shown a steady decline in median hours of sleep reported: from 7.75 in 1969 to 6.65 in 2001, with first and second year students reporting less time in bed because of earlier wake times and more erratic sleep-wake schedules92–94. In addition, in recent surveys nearly 75% of college students reported occasional sleep problems such as difficulty falling asleep, sleep disturbances, delayed sleep phase syndrome, and excessive daytime sleepiness4,95,96.

Just over a decade ago, the National Institutes of Health recognized adolescents and emerging adults (ages: 12–25 years) as a population at high risk for problem sleepiness based on "evidence that the prevalence of problem sleepiness is high and increasing with particularly serious consequences"[97]. However, relatively little systematic sleep research has focused on this critical developmental time emerging adulthood.

A well-designed study of over 1000 undergraduates' sleep-wake patterns and emotional well being by Lund et al helps fill in some of the gaps in our knowledge, regarding emerging adults' sleep and daytime functioning[86].

First, their results demonstrate that the serious problem of insufficient and erratic sleep in middle and high school age adolescents does not come to an end with graduation, but continues into the college or emerging young adult years[86].

Second, in comparing their first-year college students to the high school students surveyed in the 2006 National Sleep Foundation Sleep in America Poll or other previous studies of high school age adolescents, weeknight bedtimes and rise times appeared to be 1 hour 15 minutes later[2,86,98].

Yet, first year students had significantly later bed and rise times than older third and fourth-year college students[86]. This is a striking finding as it is in keeping with Roenneberg's work described earlier. After age 20, Roenneberg et al[87] found that mid-point times became increasingly earlier again; in other words, sleep schedules seem to become increasingly more delayed over the course of adolescence, yet this pattern seems to change by the third or fourth year of college—which generally corresponds to about ages 20–22[87].

One of the most significant factors affecting adequate sleep time and quality of sleep is a consistent sleep and wake schedule. Previous studies have determined that people who go to bed and rise at the same time each day, including the weekend, have higher quality of sleep and are less likely to report sleep deprivation[96].

In this study, the vast majority of adolescents obtained fewer than 9 hours of sleep on school nights. As our study shows During month Participants usually gone to bed was around 23.44 PM + 1.72 Hours and they wake up in morning around 7.19 AM +1.55 Hours. Over all 20.48+15.44 minute has taken to fall asleep each night. So actual sleep by participants was 7.53+1.29 hours

As Lund et al point out, few carefully designed studies have captured and articulated college-age adolescents or emerging adults' changing sleep patterns[86]. The end of adolescence is defined and/or measured by a complexity ofphysical, psychological, social, and cognitive measures.

These striking cross-sectional findings suggest a developmental change; however, they clearly need to be examined further, using a longitudinal study design and more objective measures such as polysomnography, actigraphy, salivary melatonin.

Lund et al evaluated the factors that might predict sleep quality in this sample of college students, using measures of mood, perceived distress, and substance use[86]. The transition to college may be particularly stressful for emerging adults, and developing sleep patterns may be one of the first daily habits to change for many first-year college students[94]. As Lund et al point out in the discussion of their findings, the stressors of the college years, particularly early on, may serve as ''predisposing, precipitating, and perpetuating factors'' for sleep problems at a time when sTable, less delayed sleep-wake schedules are still emerging[86].

Thus, after getting result from Present study, next will be measuring stress and its relation with sleep pattern and then giving them prescription to how to take care of stress as well as sleep problem can be done

Research Methodology

Ethical considerations: Permission to conduct the study was obtained from the Ethics Committee of the Government Medical College, Bhavnagar . Each questionnaire was accompanied by an information sheet that described the nature and purpose of the study, and explained that participation was voluntary. The respondents remained anonymous and were assured that their responses would remain confidential.

Study location and sample : This is a cross-sectional, questionnaire-based, observational study carried out from April 2016 to Aug 2017 among university students enrolled with Maharaja Krushnkumarsinji Bhavnagar University. Considering population of Bhavnagar 800000, with 99% confidence level, subject require is 664 using raosoft sample size calculator was enrolled for the study. Students were recruited for the study are from different health Professional streams: Medical, Homeopathy, Nursing and Physiotherapy college affiliated with MK Bhavnagar University. Students who were currently using sedative medications or narcotics for any acute or chronic medical condition were excluded from the study.

Confidentiality was assured to all students who were asked to volunteer and none were reimbursed. Students who were willing to participate were given a brief description about the study and its objectives. Written consent of the student was necessary for his/her enrolment. The time taken to complete the questionnaire was approximately 30-45 minutes; the student helpers subsequently collected the questionnaires. Permission to use all three instrument were obtained from copy write owner of the scale. Demographic information collected included information regarding age, sex, body mass index, Pittsburg quality of sleep index (PQSI) score, Epworth daytime sleepiness scale & Berlin Questionnaire

Instrumental tools used in the study (Annexure I)

The questionnaire includes several different types of questions about sleep habits and sleep habit and sleep apnoea. The first section contained questions about demographic characteristics: gender, age, college and body mass index (BMI).

The second section contained an 8-item questionnaire (ESS): Epworth Daytime Sleepiness Scale (EDSS)[82]: It is a scale intended to measure daytime sleepiness that is measured by use of a very short questionnaire. This can be helpful in diagnosing sleep disorders. It was introduced in 1991 by Dr. Murray Johns of Epworth Hospital in Melbourne, Australia. The questionnaire asks the subject to rate his or her probability of falling asleep on a scale of increasing probability from 0 to 3 for eight different situations. The scores for the eight questions are added together to obtain a single number. A number in the 0-9 range is considered to be normal while the numbers 10 and 11 are border line and 12-24 range indicates that expert medical advice should be sought.

Third Section was having question of Pittsburg Quality of Sleep Index (PQSI)[83]: It is a self report instrument designed to assess sleep quality during the past month and contains 19 self-rated questions from which 7 component scores are calculated and summed into a global score[99]. Higher scores represent worse sleep quality: component scores range from 0 to 3, and global scores range from 0 to 21. It analyze factors such as sleep quality, sleep latency, sleep duration, sleep efficiency, sleep disturbance and use of sleep medication.

This Index is an internationally recognised instrument used to evaluate sleep behaviours in the preceding month[84] It entails 19 items and has a reliability coefficient (Cronbach's alpha) of 0.83 for its seven components.9 Numerous studies using the PSQI have supported its high validity and reliability.10-12 The total PSQI score ranges from 0 to 21; higher scores reflect poorer quality of sleep. In general, a PSQI score of higher than 5 is considered to indicate poor sleep quality[15,84].

Forth Section Was having total 10 question (Berlin Questionnaire)[85]: Berlin Questionnaire (BQ): The BQ is a screening tool used widely for the identification of Subject who may be at high risk for OSA. Subjects can be divided in high risk and low risk of OSA based on responses to symptom questions grouped in three categories. They will be considered to be at high risk for sleep apnea if 2 of the 3 following criteria were met: 1) snoring with two of the following features: louder than talking, at least 3 to 4 times a week, complaints by others about snoring, witnessed breathing pauses at least 3 to 4 times a week; 2) early morning and daytime fatigue exceeding 3 to 4 times a week or having fallen asleep while driving; and 3) presence of hypertension or obesity. Prior approval from respective copy write holder of scale was taken and also translated from English to Gujarati language, it was retranslated for correctness of translation as well as validated and the reliability of the instrument was established.

Statistical analysis:

All data were coded, entered, and then analyzed using the Graph Pad. Descriptive results were expressed as frequency, percentage, and mean ± S.D. P-valus < 0.05 were accepted as statistically significant. A difference in means between groups was carried out using independent sample t test and ANOVA.

Result

In Present study we have studied response of total 664 participants studying in various health professional streams under Maharaja Krishnakumarsinhji University. Demographic details of participants are as follow:

Age: In Present study participants were between 16-30 years with highest 36.3% subject with age of 18-19.

Figure: 1

Age Distribution of Participants

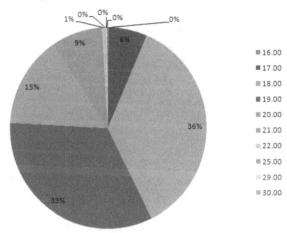

Gender: 34.3% Male and 65.7% Female

Figure: 2

Distribution of Participants Based on Stream

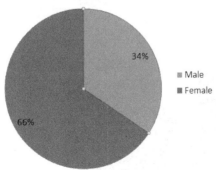

Stream : We have students from different stream studying in health professional institute affiliated to university . Study group was consist of 23% BHMS, 21.1% BPT, 29.1% MBBS, 26.8% Nursing students.

Figure: 3

Distribution of Participants Based on Stream

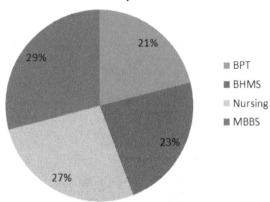

BMI : Average BMI of the participates were 21.7 ± 5.0 kg/m^2 with Average height of 159.17 ± 12.32 cm and Average weight of 54.25 ± 9.75 Kg {OVERWEIGHT(BMI:23-24.99), PREOBESE(BMI:25-29.99), GRADE 1 OBESITY(BMI:30-34.99), GRADE 2 OBESITY(BMI:35-39.99), GRADE 3 OBESITY(BMI>40)}

Figure: 4

Distribution of Participants Based on BMI

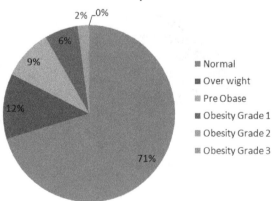

Detailed analysis of Pittsburgh quality of sleep index (PQSI) score, Epworth daytime sleepiness scale & Berlin Questionnaire. Participants response to above Questionnaire are mention in below Tables.

Epworth daytime sleepiness scale: In Table 5 to Table 13 below we can see response of participants based on rating scale for dozing in different conditions.

Table No 5: Dozing During Sitting and Reading

	Frequency	Percent
Would never Doze	114	17.2
Slight Chance of Dozing	330	49.7
Moderate Chance of Dozing	161	24.2
High Chance of Dozing	59	8.9
Total	664	100

Figure:5
Dozing During Sitting and Reading

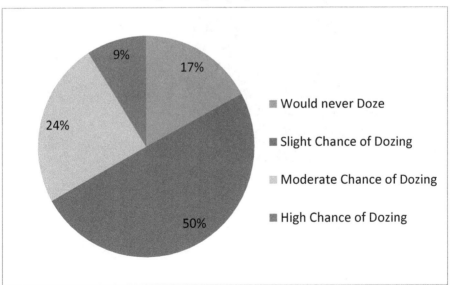

Table No 6: Dozing During Watching TV

	Frequency	Percent
Would never Doze	431	64.9
Slight Chance of Dozing	183	27.6
Moderate Chance of Dozing	35	5.3
High Chance of Dozing	15	2.3
Total	664	100

Figure:6
Dozing During Watching TV

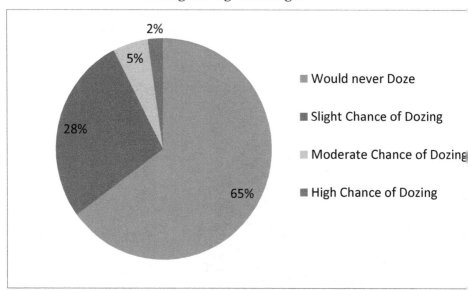

Table No 7: Dozing During Sitting in active in public place , during lecture or at meeting

	Frequency	Percent
Would never Doze	351	52.9
Slight Chance of Dozing	221	33.3
Moderate Chance of Dozing	67	10.1
High Chance of Dozing	25	3.8
Total	664	100

Figure:7

Dozing During Sitting in active in public palce , during lecture or at meeting

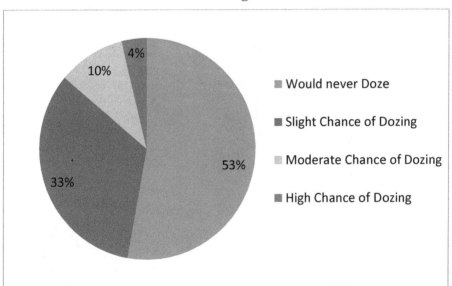

Table No 8: Dozing as a pasagner in a care for an hour without break

	Frequency	Percent
Would never Doze	167	25.2
Slight Chance of Dozing	225	33.9
Moderate Chance of Dozing	193	29.1
High Chance of Dozing	79	11.9
Total	664	100

Figure:8

Dozing as a pasagner in a care for an hour without break

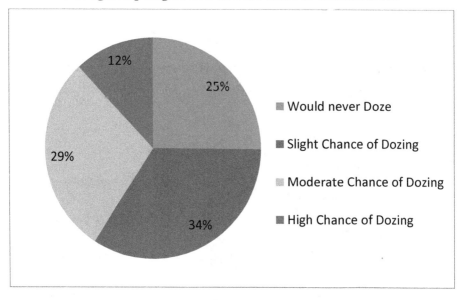

Table No : 9: Dozing During lying down at rest in the afternoon when circumstances permit

	Frequency	Percent
Would never Doze	88	13.3
Slight Chance of Dozing	183	27.6
Moderate Chance of Dozing	177	26.7
High Chance of Dozing	216	32.5
Total	664	100

Figure:9

Dozing During lying down at rest in the afternoon when circumstances permit

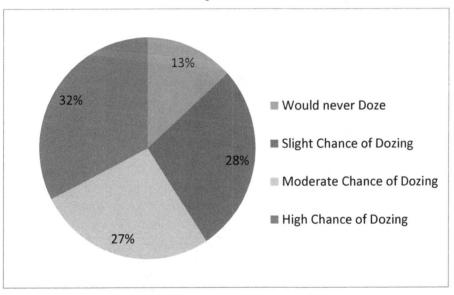

Table No 10: Dozing During Sitting and talking with some one

	Frequency	Percent
Would never Doze	574	86.4
Slight Chance of Dozing	77	11.6
Moderate Chance of Dozing	11	1.7
High Chance of Dozing	2	0.3
Total	664	100

Figure:10

Dozing During Sitting and talking with some one

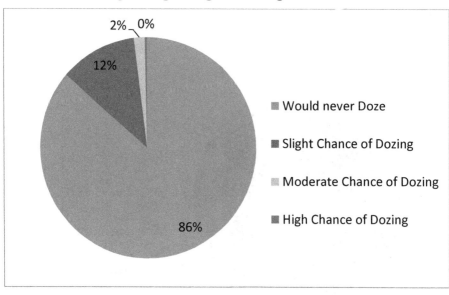

Table No 11: Dozing During Sitting after lunch

	Frequency	Percent
	1	0.2
Would never Doze	179	27
Slight Chance of Dozing	273	41.1
Moderate Chance of Dozing	132	19.9
High Chance of Dozing	79	11.9
Total	664	100

Figure:11

Dozing During Sitting after lunch

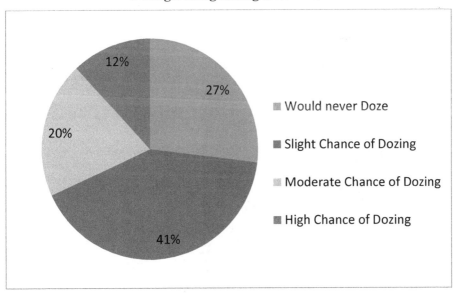

Table No 12: Dozing in a care while stopped for a few minutes in traffic

	Frequency	Percent
Would never Doze	606	91.3
Slight Chance of Dozing	47	7.1
Moderate Chance of Dozing	8	1.2
High Chance of Dozing	3	0.5
Total	664	100

Figure: 12

Dozing in a care while stopped for a few minutes in traffic

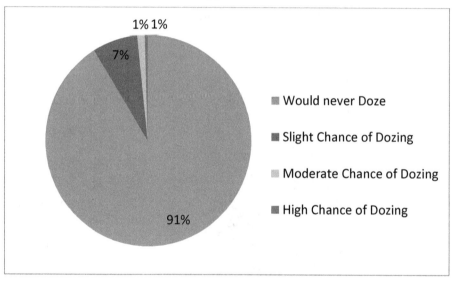

Table No 13: Distribution based on
Total Epworth Daytime Sleepiness Scale Score

		Frequency	Percent
Less than 10	Most likely getting enough sleep	562	84.6
10 - 15	May be suffering from excessive daytime sleepiness	96	14.5
16+	Dangerously sleepy	6	1

Figure: 13
Distribution based on
Total Epworth Daytime Sleepiness Scale Score

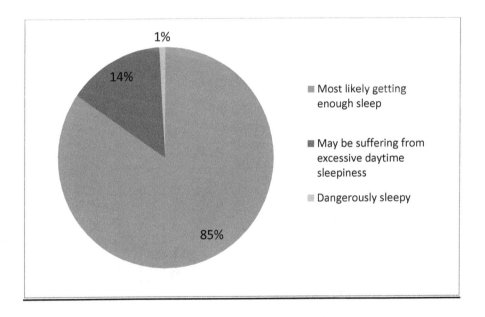

Pittsburgh quality of sleep index (PQSI) score

In Table 14 to 22 Table below we can see response of participants based on PQSI rating scale.

Table No 14: Time to go to bed in last Month

	Frequency	Percent
0	6	.9
1	99	14.9
2	36	5.4
3	12	1.8
4	4	.6
21	4	.6
22	38	5.7
23	196	29.5
24	269	40.5
Total	664	100

Table No 15: Time of waking up doing last month (Clock)

	Frequency	Percent
0	1	.2
2	1	.2
3	5	.8
4	4	.6
5	37	5.6
6	137	20.6
7	216	32.5
8	184	27.7
9	54	8.1
10	16	2.4

11	5	.8
12	1	.2
Total	664	100

Table No 16 : Time taken to fall asleep after going in bed (in minute)

	Frequency	Percent
1 to 10	259	39.0
11 to 20	214	32.2
21 to 30	137	20.6
31 to 40	13	1.9
41 to 50	10	1.5
51 to 60	22	3.3
> 60	9	1.3
Total	664	100

Figure: 14

Time taken to fall asleep after going in bed (in minute)

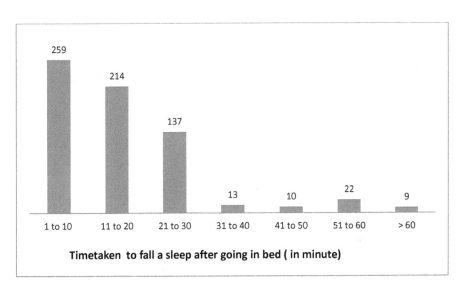

Table No 17: Actual hour of sleep did you got in last month

	Frequency	Percent
0	1	.2
3	1	.2
4	3	.5
5	37	5.6
6	110	16.6
7	203	30.6
8	214	32.2
9	61	9.2
10	23	3.5
11	1	.2
12	5	.8
13	1	.2
Total	664	100

Table No 18: During the past month, how often have you had trouble sleeping because you

	Not during the past month	Less than once a week	once or twice a week	Three or more times a week
a. Cannot get to sleep within 30 minutes	51.8	18.8	18.5	10.8
b. Wake up in the middle of the night or early morning	46.8	23.3	17.9	11.9
c. Have to get up to use the bathroom	62.2	16.4	13.4	8.0
d. Cannot breathe comfortably	90.7	4.4	4.1	0.9
e. Cough or snore loudly	89.5	6.2	3.0	1.4

f. Feel too cold	74.4	16.1	6.2	3.2
g. Feel too hot	58.7	18.1	10.4	12.7
h. Have bad dreams	63.3	22.6	9.9	4.2
i. Have pain	81.0	8.1	6.0	4.7

Table No 19: During the past month how often have you taken medicine prescribed

	Frequency	Percent
Not During the Past Month	641	96.5
less than once a week During the Past Month	11	1.7
once or twice a week During the Past Month	6	0.9
three or four times a week During the Past Month	6	0.9
Total	664	100

Figure: 15

During the past month how often have you taken medicine prescribed

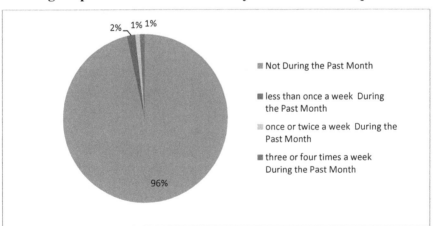

Table No 20: During the past month, how often have you had trouble staying awake while driving, eating meals, or engaging in social activity

	Frequency	Percent
Not During the Past Month	558	84
less than once a week During the Past Month	88	13.3
once or twice a week During the Past Month	13	2
three or four times a week During the Past Month	5	0.8
Total	664	100

Figure:16

During the past month, how often have you had trouble staying awake while driving, eating meals, or engaging in social activity

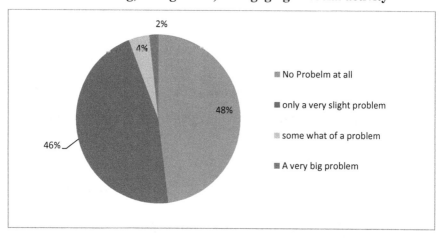

Table No 21: During the past month, how much of a problem has it been for you to keep up enthusiasm to get things done?

	Frequency	Percent
No Problem at all	319	48
only a very slight problem	306	46.1
somewhat of a problem	27	4.1
A very big problem	12	1.8
Total	664	100

Figure:17

During the past month, how much of a problem has it been for you to keep up enthusiasm to get things done?

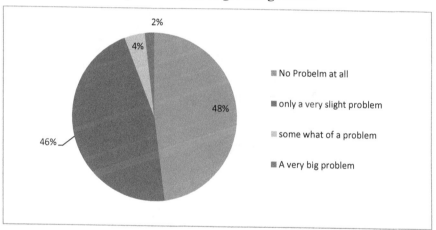

Table No 22: During the past month how would you rate your sleep quality overall

	Frequency	Percent
Very good	209	31.5
fairly good	387	58.3
Fairly Bad	53	8
Very bad	15	2.3
Total	664	100

Figure: 18

During the past month how would you rate your sleep quality overall

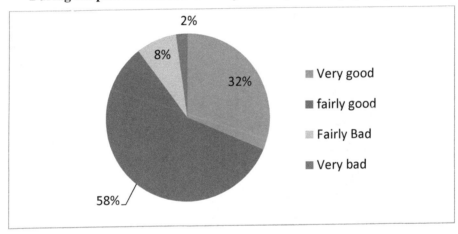

Based on seven Component Quality of Sleep amongst participants are shown in Table 23 to 30

Table No 23: PSQIDURAT (Duration of sleep)

	Frequency	Percent
Better sleep	512	77.1
Good sleep	110	16.6
Average Sleep	37	5.6
Worst sleep	5	0.8
Total	664	100

Table No 24: PSQIDISTB (Sleep Disturbance)

	Frequency	Percent
Better sleep	97	14.6
Good sleep	466	70.2
Average Sleep	98	14.8
Worst sleep	3	0.5
Total	664	100

Table No 25: PSQILATEN (Sleep Latency)

	Frequency	Percent
Better sleep	195	29.4
Good sleep	331	49.8
Average Sleep	132	19.9
Worst sleep	6	0.9
Total	664	100

Table No 26: PSQISLPQUAL (Overall Sleep Quality)

	Frequency	Percent
Better sleep	209	31.5
Good sleep	387	58.3
Average Sleep	53	8
Worst sleep	15	2.3
Total	664	100

Table No 27: PSQIMEDS (Need Medicines To Sleep)

	Frequency	Percent
Better sleep	641	96.5
Good sleep	11	1.7
Average Sleep	6	0.9
Worst sleep	6	0.9
Total	664	100

Table No 28 : PSQIDAYDYS (Day Dysfunction Due To Sleepiness)

	Frequency	Percent
Better sleep	275	41.4
Good sleep	356	53.6
Average Sleep	30	4.5
Worst sleep	3	0.5
Total	664	100

Table No 29 : PSQIHSE (Sleep Efficiency)

	Frequency	Percent
Better sleep	614	92.5
Good sleep	31	4.7
Average Sleep	12	1.8
Worst sleep	7	1.1
Total	664	100

Table No 30: Over all Sleep Quality based on PSQI Scale

	Frequency	Percent
Good Sleep Quality	593	89.3
Poor Sleep Quality	71	10.7
Total	664	100

Figure: 19

Over all Sleep Quality based on PSQI Scale

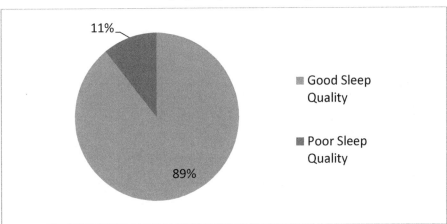

Berlin Questionnaire:

Berlin score of participants are shown in Table No 31 to 40 .Below. In respect to Berlin Questionnaire, which identify people who are at high risk to sleep apnoea syndrome revels following characteristics: 0.9% cases, people have noticed it daily, 1.2% cases it happens 3-4 times a week and in 4.8% it happens daily and in rest of the case 92.9% case it never occurs. Out of all participants 8.9% feels tired or fatigue after sleep every day and Out of all 8.1% felts tired during waking time. Only 2.0% responded that they nodded off or fallen asleep during driving vehicle. Overall berline score was positive in 2.4% cases suggestive of need of medical intervention and consultation with sleep expert

Table No 31: Snoring amongst Participants

	Frequency	Percent
Yes Snore	24	3.6
No Snore	571	86
Do not know	69	10.4
Total	664	100

Table No 32: Loudness of Snoring

	Frequency	Percent
Slightly louder than breathing	21	3.2
As loud as talking	2	.3
Loud	1	.2
Total	24	100

Table No 33: How often do you snore

	Frequency	Percent
Almost every day	1	.2
3-4 times per week	4	.6
1-2 times per week	13	2.0
1-2 times per month	6	.9
Total	24	100

Table No 34: Has your snoring ever bothered other people

	Frequency	Percent
Yes	7	1.1
No	14	2.1
Do not know	3	.5
Total	24	100

Table No 35: Has anyone noticed that quit breathing during you sleep

	Frequency	Percent
Almost every day	6	0.9
3-4 times per week	8	1.2
1-2 times per week	32	4.8
1-2 times per month	618	93.1
Total	664	100

Table No 36: How often do you feel tired or fatigued after you sleep

	Frequency	Percent
Almost every day	59	8.9
3-4 times per week	41	6.2
1-2 times per week	233	35.1
1-2 times per month	331	49.9
Total	664	100

Table No 37: During your waking time do you feel tired fatigued

	Frequency	Percent
Almost every day	54	8.1
3-4 times per week	46	6.9
1-2 times per week	243	36.6
1-2 times per month	321	48.4
Total	664	100

Table No 38: Have you ever nodded off or fallen asleep while driving a vehicle

	Frequency	Percent
Yes	13	2
No	651	98.1
Total	664	100

Table No 39: Do you have high blood pressure

	Frequency	Percent
Yes	14	2.1
No	602	90.7
Do not know	48	7.3
Total	664	100

Table No 40: Berlin Positive

	Frequency	Percent
Berlin Positive	16	2.4
Berlin Negative	648	97.6
Total	664	100

Figure:20
Berlin Positive

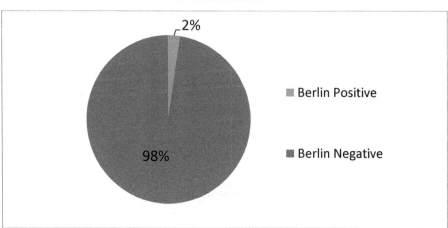

Detailed History of 16 burlin Subjects was done after decoding of response was taken one to one and out of which one subject was found positive, thus Polysomnography Was done for that subject. Result of the same is summarised here

Polysomnography was conducted on the night of 06-12-2017. The following v monitored: central and occipital EEG, electrooculogram (EOG), submentalis El nasal and oral airflow, thoracic and abdominal wall motion, anterior tibialis El body position and electrocardiogram. Arterial oxygen saturation was monitored wi pulse oximcter. The tracing was scored using 30 second epochs. Hypopneas v scored per AASM definition

Sleep Summary

Lights Out:	23:09:30	Stage	Duration	% TST
Lights On:	06:49:30	N1	109.5 min	78.2%
Total Recording Time:	460.0 min	N2	17.0 min	12.1%
Total Sleep Time (TST):	140.0 min	N3	5.5 min	3.9%
Sleep Period Time:	460.0 min	R	8.0 min	5.7%
Sleep Onset:	23:09:30			
Sleep Efficiency:	30.4 %	Latencies	From Lights Out	From .
Sleep Latency (from LOff):	0.0 min	N1	13.5 min	13.5 n
R Latency (from Sleep Onset):	14.0 min	N2	182.0 min	182.0
Wake After Sleep Onset	320.0 min	N3	0.0 min	0.0 mi
Wake During Sleep:	320.0 min	R	14.0	14.0
Total Wake Time:	320.0 min			
% Wake Time:	69.6			

Respiratory Summary

By Event Classification	Central			Mixed			Obstructive	
	Count	Mean	Max	Count	Mea	Max	Coun	Mean
Apneas, NREM	3	55.7	138.0	3	15.2	22.5	26	18.3
Apneas, REM	0	0.0	0.0	0	0.0	0.0	0	0.0
Apneas, Total	3	55.7	138.0	3	15.2	22.5	26	18.3
*Hypopneas scored based on 0% or greater desaturation.								
Hypopneas, NREM	83	20.2	52.0	RERAs, NREM	0	0.0		
Hypopneas, REM	3	12.8	16.0	RERAs, REM	0	0.0		
Hypopneas, Total	86	19.9	52.0	RERAs, Total	0	0.0		
Event Statistics	Total			With Arousal				

	Count	Index		Count	Index
Apneas, Total	32	13.7		11	4.7
Hypopneas, Total	86	36.9		43	18.4
Apnea + Hypopnea Total	118	**AHI: 50.6**		54	23.1
Apnea + Hypopnea NREM	115	**AHI: 52.3**		48	21.8
Apnea + Hypopnea REM	3	**AHI: 22.5**		4	30.0
RERAs, Total	0	0.0		0	0.0
Total Events (A+H+RERA)	118	**RDI: 50.6**		54	23.1
Total Events (A+H+RERA)	115	**RDI: 52.3**		48	21.8
Total Events (A+H+RERA)	3	**RDI: 22.5**		4	30.0

Hypoventilation: None Present

Respiratory Summary by Body Position											
By Body Positio	Back	Left	Righ	Pron	Tota		Back	Left	Right	Pron	Tota
Apn Index, REM					0.0	AHI,					22.5
Apn Index, NRE					14.5	AHI,					52.3
Apn Index, Total					13.7	AHI,					50.6
Hyp Index, REM					22.5	RDI,					22.5
Hyp Index, NRE					37.7	RDI,					52.3
Hyp Index, Total					36.9	RDI, Total					50.6
Duration (min)					460.	TST (min)					460.

Heart Rate Summary	
Average Heart Rate During Sleep	85.3 bpm
Highest Heart Rate During Sleep	255 bpm
Highest Heart Rate During Sleep 95th %	105.0 bpm
Highest Heart Rate During Recording (TIB)	255 bpm
Highest Heart Rate During Recording (TIB) 95th %	99.0 bpm

Heart Rate Observations		
Event Type	# Events	
Bradycardia	0	Lowest HR Scored: N/A
Sinus Tachycardia During	0	Highest HR Scored: N/A
Narrow Complex Tachycardia	0	Highest HR Scored: N/A
Wide Complex Tachycardia	0	Highest HR Scored: N/A
Asystole	0	Longest Pause: N/A
Atrial Fibrillation	0	Duration Longest Event: N/A
Other Arrythmias	Yes or No	Description:

Arousals					
	Total #	Respiratory	Limb Movement	Snore	Spontaneous
REM	11	4	0	0	7
NREM	127	48	0	16	63
WAKE	5	2	0	1	2
TOTAI	143	54	0	17	72
INDEX	61.3	23.1	0.0	7.3	30.9

# of Snore Arousals:	17
Snore Arousal Index:	7.3
# of Snore Episodes:	122
Total duration w/ snoring:	11.4 min

Oximetry Data				
Average O2 while	99 %	Average O2 while in Non-		99 %
Average O2 while in	98 %	Approximate minimum O2		78 %

	WK	REM	NREM	Total
<50 % (min)	0.0	0.0	0.0	0.0
<60 % (min)	0.0	0.0	0.0	0.0
<70 % (min)	0.0	0.0	0.0	0.0
<75 % (min)	0.0	0.0	0.0	0.0
<80 % (min)	0.0	0.0	0.0	0.0
<85 % (min)	0.0	0.0	0.0	0.0
<90 % (min)	0.2	0.0	0.1	0.3
<95 % (min)	0.7	0.0	0.2	0.9
<0 % (min)				
Fail (min)	8.2	0.0	7.1	15.3
Average (%)	99	98	99	99
Desat Index (#/hour)		0.0	9.1	8.6
Desat Max (%)	3	0	12	12
Desat Max Dur (sec)	5.0	0.0	17.0	17.0
Oximetry Summary				
	W	R	NR	Total
Fail Duration (min)	8.2	0.0	7.1	15.3
Average (%)	99	98	99	99
# of Desaturations*	1	0	19	19
Desat Index (#/hour)		0.0	9.1	8.6
Desat Max Dur	5.0	0.0	17.0	17.0

*Desaturations based on 3% or greater drop from baseline.
Minimum SpO2 value during sleep: 78%
Minimum SpO2 value duration during sleep: 3 seconds
Minimum SpO2 value associated with a respiratory event: 78%

The result is suggestive of very sever OSA. Thus he was advised to use Continuous positive airway pressure devise.

Discussion

College prepares an individual to face the challenges in professional and personal life. Quality of sleep also impacts the physical health, mental health and quality of life of University students.

Good quality sleep is pertinent for the health and wellbeing of an individual. It is a key for next day freshness, energy, enthusiasm and saneness. Depth, restfulness of sleep and feeling freshness after awakening are some of the salient characteristic of sleep quality. Good sleep is unbroken, uneventful, has short latency and has no awakening throughout[99].

Poor sleep quality and insomnia symptoms have been associated with worse health, increased health care costs and utilization, absenteeism from work, and increased risk for psychiatric disorders, including depression[99].

Daytime sleepiness has been associated with increased risk of motor vehicle accidents, worse physical health, and increased mortality risk[100]. This study aimed to describe the sleep Pattern among university students in Bhavnagar. Although sleep and sleepiness can be measured by objective means such as polysomnography (PSG) and the multiple sleep latency test (MSLT), these methods are often impractical as clinical screening or research tools.

Self-report questionnaires are most commonly used to assess sleep quality and daytime sleepiness. Many different instruments have been developed to measure sleep quality, insomnia, and daytime sleepiness, but 2 of the most widely-used are the Pittsburgh Sleep Quality Index (PSQI)4 and the Epworth Sleepiness Scale (ESS).[101,102]. Similarly, The Berlin questionnaire (BQ), developed in 1999 by Netzer and colleadues in United States, is one of the most popular questionnaires for screening OSA[24,85].

In present study we used this three questionnaire to find our sleep pattern among university students. In present study 16 students (2.4%) out of total 664 reported to have poor sleep quality. This is in contrast to other studies that 62.6% of the Indian under graduate students had poor sleep quality[103].

Almost similar data is reported from Malaysian university students,. Studies in Chinese, Thai, Taiwanese, Ethiopian, Lebanese, Chilean and American college students reported that 40- 55% of students had poor sleep quality. Prevalence of poor sleep quality was almost double in Taiwanese, Lebanese and Ethiopian college students than study population. A substantial portion (96.4%) of the Brazilian college students also had poor sleep quality[103].

In Present study daytime sleepiness with High chance of dozing was observed in 0.3 to 32.5 of participants with maximum during

Lying down to rest in the afternoon. This high level amongst all reason may be attributed to local cultural of taking nap after lunch in afternoon. Only 2.3% of participants reported overall bed sleep quality. In coming section we are trying discuss Gender wise, stream wise or BMI wise difference in sleep pattern.

In following data, Pearson Chi Square was conducted for data superscript with **a**, which are not differ significantly from each other at the .05 level. **b** denotes data Computed only for a 2x2 table

Table-41. Sleep pattern according to Gender amongst University students: Gender v/s Epworth Sleepiness Scale

			EP			Total
			Most likely getting enough sleep	May be suffering from excessive daytime sleepiness	Dangerously sleepy	
Gender	Male	Count	207_a	20_b	$1_{a,b}$	228
		% within Gender	90.8%	8.8%	0.4%	100.0%
	Female	Count	355_a	76_b	$5_{a,b}$	436
		% within Gender	81.4%	17.4%	1.1%	100.0%
Total		Count	562	96	6	664
		% within Gender	84.6%	14.5%	0.9%	100.0%

Table above suggest that out of all participants 8.8% of Male maybe suffering from excessive daytime sleepiness and only 0.4% were felling dangerously sleepy which is low in compare to female participants with 17.4% suffering from excessive daytime sleepiness and 1.14% were felling dangerously sleepy. Our result are similar with the previous study[103].

A female predominance of sleeping complaints has been found in many previous epidemiologic surveys. When the self-reported sleeping time for men and women was compared, a highly significant difference was found. On average, women normally slept 22 minutes longer each night. This is in accordance with data found by Bliwise et al[104] and by Broman et al[105]. However, despite the longer sleeping time, women suffered from a higher degree of lack of sleep than men. The mean difference between the reported need for sleep and total sleep time among females was 56 minutes compared to 40 minutes for males ($p < 0.05$). When defining insomnia as the chronic inability to obtain the amount of sleep that a person needs for optimal functioning and well-being [106], it seems clear from the data obtained that females constitute a risk group. Due to the higher degree of lack of sleep, it is not surprising that the prevalence of daytime sleepiness and the absence of feeling refreshed in the morning are significantly higher among females. In addition to the lack of sleep, females also reported more awakenings/night

Physiological reasons for gender differences in sleeping patterns: Physiologic changes in neuroendocrine hormones, body temperature, mood, and emotional state during puberty, the menstrual cycle, pregnancy, and menopause have profound effects on sleep quality, daytime functioning, and well-being in adolescent girls and adult women. It generally has been assumed that sleep prior to puberty is similar in girls and boys, and that sex differences first emerge during this developmental transition. However, since scientific studies have focused primarily on men, rather than women, the scientific basis for this assumption has not yet been established.

A recent study at the University of Pennsylvania found that individuals with higher socioeconomic status and education levels sleep better than those of lower socioeconomic status. The study also found that gender, younger age and being single negatively affect sleep. Women reported more sleep problems than men (22 percent versus 16 percent), especially between the ages of 40 and 65 years. Finally, more sleep problems were reported in people between the ages of 18 and 24 years than older people.

Insomnia : Insomnia is a condition of poor quality sleep: such as, for example, trouble falling asleep, waking up early or feeling un rested after a full night's sleep. This occurs more often in women than in men and may be related to depression or other emotional complications. There is some research to suggest that insomnia and related symptoms may be associated with onset of menses.

Insomnia related to menses may be related to a decrease in endogenous progesterone or a differential sensitivity to endogenous hormone fluctuations. Potential health consequences or disease risk that may result from this repetitive 'incident' insomnia that can occur every month for 40 years of a woman's life are not known[107,108].

Sleep Apnoea: Sleep Apnoea describes a condition where breathing is paused when tissue in the back of the throat collapses and blocks the airway as you sleep. This occurs in about two percent of women. In a research study carried out on rats, researchers at the University of Wisconsin-Madison discovered that levels of oestrogen and serotonin affects breathing, with important consequences for sleep Apnoea. More men, especially middle-aged men, suffer from sleep apnoea; possibly as a result of the different hormonal balance.

Women usually complain about difficulties in falling asleep[109], while men have more problems in sleep maintenance, lighter sleep, and more frequent sleep-related breathing disorders[110]. More recent studies also revealed gender differences in the sleep EEG. Differences between men and women were suggested in terms of brain maturation, perceived sleep, NREM–REM distribution, or EEG features[111-116].

Gender effect was stronger for younger subjects, with women going to bed and falling asleep earlier, and sleeping longer. Reported sleep latency increased in women with aging (70–80 year versus 40–49 years group, and 70–80 years versus 50–59 years group, P 0.001). Sleep efficiency decreased both in men and women with aging, with 40–49 years and 50–59 years groups having higher sleep efficiency than the other two groups. The presence of sleep disturbances was highest in 50–59 years women and lowest in the oldest women (P 0.05). The gender effect was stronger in the youngest population, with women going earlier to sleep compared with men, but these differences dissipate with age[107,108].

The ESS should not be considered the definitive or only measure for assessing daytime sleepiness, particularly for women. For example, based on the unadjusted OR in this study, women would be 38% less likely to have an abnormal ESS score and 44% more likely to report feeling under stressed than would men. Clinically, if these measures are used to identify sleepiness in men and women, large differences in the percentage of men or women would be identified depending on which measure is used.

Table No 42. Gender V/s Berlin Questionnaire

			BQ		Total
			No	Yes	
Gender	Male	Count	221a	7a	228
		% within Gender	96.9%	3.1%	100.0%
	Female	Count	427a	9a	436
		% within Gender	97.9%	2.1%	100.0%
Total		Count	648	16	664
		% within Gender	97.6%	2.4%	100.0%

Table above suggest that out of all only 3.1% male were having chance of

obstructive sleep apnoea compare to 2.1% female participants having chance of

OSA. This gender difference in OSA may be attributed to physical difference in

the gender.

The biological mechanisms underpinning the gender-related differences in OSA

prevalence remain incompletely understood. The explanations proposed to date

include the protective effects of female hormones on fat deposition, the

chemical drive to breathe, and leptin levels, as well as the greater airway

collapsibility seen in men.6,7 As a result of the association between OSA and

aging,8 women at postmenopausal 6,7,8. age and men may have a similar

prevalence of OSA.

Indeed, Few Study found slightly higher OSA prevalence among women than

men. the absence of male predominance in our cohort[117] of cardiac patients is the result of the differing demographic and risk factor profiles of individuals seen in the community and in sleep clinics. suggests hormonal change associated with menopause is a likely explanation for the lack of sex predilection observed in our study. Aging has been shown to be an important risk factor for OSA owing to the age-related increase in fat deposition in the parapharyngeal area, lengthening of the soft palate, and changes in the body structures surrounding the pharynx.

Moreover, in postmenopausal women, the loss of 25,26 progesterone and estrogens also lead to changes in respiratory control and functional control of the upper airway that predisposes them to OSA

Table No.43. Gender v/s Pittsburgh Quality of Sleep Index

			PSQI		Total
			Good sleep quality	Poor sleep quality	
Gender	Male	Count	204a	24a	228
		% within Gender	89.5%	10.5%	100.0%
	Fem ale	Count	390a	46a	436
		% within Gender	89.4%	10.6%	100.0%
Total		Count	594	70	664
		% within Gender	89.5%	10.5%	100.0%

When it comes to poor sleep quality no gender difference is seen as 10.5% Male and 10.6% Female reported poor sleep quality. It can be postulated that this similarity can be natural as more daytime sleepiness was observed in female and more chances of OSA was observed in Female so combination of both condition attributing to equal no of gender reporting poor sleep quality.

Table No : 44. Gender V/S Duration of sleep

			PSQIDURAT				
			Duration Of Sleep >7 Hr	Duration Of Sleep < 7 And > 6	Duration Of Sleep < 6 And > 5	Duration Of Sleep <5 Hr	Total
Gender	Male	Count	181a	36a	10a	1a	228
		% within Gender	79.4%	15.8%	4.4%	0.4%	100.0%
	Female	Count	331a	74a	27a	4a	436
		% within Gender	75.9%	17.0%	6.2%	0.9%	100.0%
Total		Count	512	110	37	5	5
		% within Gender	77.1%	16.6%	5.6%	0.8%	0.8%

Gender difference on different component of PSQI suggest that on an average 90% university students are getting sleep more than 6 hours. With moderate to excessive sleep disturbance observe only in 15% case (). Sleep latency was observed more in male compare to female participants with overall more than one hour latency was observed in 2% cases.

Table No: 45.Gender V/S Sleep Disturbance

			\multicolumn{5}{c}{PSQIDISTB}				
			No Sleep Disturbance	Little Sleep Disturbance	More Sleep Disturbance	Excessive Sleep Disturbance	T
Gender	Male	Count	54a	151b	23b	0a, b	
		% within Gender	23.7%	66.2%	10.1%	0.0%	10
	Female	Count	43a	315b	75b	3a, b	
		% within Gender	9.9%	72.2%	17.2%	0.7%	10
Total		Count	97	466	98	3	
		% within Gender	14.6%	70.2%	14.8%	0.5%	10

Table No: 46. Gender V/S Sleep Latency

			\multicolumn{5}{c}{PSQILATEN}				
			Sleep Latency > 0 and < 15 min	Sleep Latency > 15 and < 30 min	Sleep Latency > 30 and < 60 min	Sleep Latency > 60 min	Tota
Gender	Male	Count	63_a	107_a	55_a	3_a	228
		% within Gender	27.6%	46.9%	24.1%	1.3%	100
	Female	Count	132_a	224_a	77_a	3_a	436
		% within Gender	30.3%	51.4%	17.7%	0.7%	100.
Total		Count	195	331	132	6	664
		% within Gender	29.4%	49.8%	19.9%	0.9%	100

Based in PSQI response only 8% participants were having poor sleep quality with female predominance, while worst sleep quality was observed in 2.3%

cases with Male predominance. Less than 1% participats needed medicine for

getting sleep

Table No: 47. Gender V/S Overall Sleep Quality

			PSQISLPQUAL				
			Better SLEEP QUALITY	Good SLEEP QUALITY	Poor SLEEP QUALITY	Worst SLEEP QUALITY	Total
Gender	Male	Count	84$_a$	125$_{a,b}$	12$_b$	7$_{a,b}$	228
		% within Gender	36.8%	54.8%	5.3%	3.1%	100.0%
	Female	Count	125$_a$	262$_{a,b}$	41$_b$	8$_{a,b}$	436
		% within Gender	28.7%	60.1%	9.4%	1.8%	100.0%
Total		Count	209	387	53	15	664
		% within Gender	31.5%	58.3%	8.0%	2.3%	100.0%

Table No: 48. Gender V/S Need Medicine to Sleep

			PSQIMEDS				
			No Medicine during the past month	less than once Medicine during the past week	once or twice Medicine during the past week	three to four times Medicine during the past week	Total
Gender	Male	Count	218$_a$	4$_{a,b}$	5$_b$	1$_a$	228
		% within Gender	95.6%	1.8%	2.2%	0.4%	100.0%
	Female	Count	423$_a$	7$_{a,b}$	1$_b$	5$_a$	436
		% within Gender	97.0%	1.6%	0.2%	1.1%	100.0%
Total		Count	641	11	6	6	664
		% within Gender	96.5%	1.7%	0.9%	0.9%	100.0%

Most of the participants were having more than 75% sleep efficiency. Dysfunction due to sleep disturbance in daily routine was observed only in 5% cases. .

Table No: 49. Gender V/S Sleep Efficiency

			PSQIHSE				
			SLEEP EFFICIENCY > 85	SLEEP EFFICIENCY < 85 and > 75,	SLEEP EFFICIENCY < 75 and > 65,	SLEEP EFFICIENCY < 65,	To
Gender	Male	Count	213_a	7_a	4_a	4_a	22
		% within Gender	93.4%	3.1%	1.8%	1.8%	10(
	Female	Count	401_a	24_a	8_a	3_a	43(
		% within Gender	92.0%	5.5%	1.8%	0.7%	10(
Total		Count	614	31	12	7	66
		% within Gender	92.5%	4.7%	1.8%	1.1%	10(

Analyses exploring the differential effect of various risk factors on sleep quality suggest that most of the lifestyle factors (eg, smoking, drug abuse) seem to exhibit gender specific association. Due to the cross-sectional nature of the

study, it could not be said whether unhealthy lifestyle preceded sleep quality, or poor sleep quality affected lifestyle. However, considering the study subjects were very young, it may not be unlikely that unhealthy lifestyle preceded poor sleep quality. Our results uphold previous findings of poor sleep in the minority population on sleep problems in young adults,29 though evidence from longitudinal studies is needed to explore the differential effect seen in our study.

Table No: 50. Gender V/S Day Dysfunction Due To Sleepiness

			PSQIDAYS				
			Dysfunction Due To Sleepiness : 0 Day	Dysfunction Due To Sleepiness : > 1 And < 2 Day	Dysfunction Due To Sleepiness : > 3 And < 4 Day	Dysfunction Due To Sleepiness : > 5 And < 6 Day	Total
Gender	Male	Count	100_a	119_a	8_a	1_a	228
		% within Gender	43.9%	52.2%	3.5%	0.4%	100.0%
	Female	Count	175_a	237_a	22_a	2_a	436
		% within Gender	40.1%	54.4%	5.0%	0.5%	100.0%
Total		Count	275	356	30	3	664
		% within Gender	41.4%	53.6%	4.5%	0.5%	100.0%

Following Table shows that there is no major difference between different streams under study in reference to day time sleepiness. Less than 5 hours of sleep was observed only in BPT Students and only 56% students shows having more than 7 hours of sleep, followed by 69.1% in nursing students.

Table No: 51. Stream V/S Epworth Daytime Sleepiness Scale

			EP			Total
			Most likely getting enough sleep	May be suffering from excessive daytime sleepiness	Dangerously sleepy	
Stream	BPT	Count	121_a	17_a	2_a	140
		% within Stream	86.4%	12.1%	1.4%	100.0%
	BHMS	Count	133_a	19_a	1_a	153
		% within Stream	86.9%	12.4%	0.7%	100.0%
	Nursing	Count	144_a	32_a	2_a	178
		% within Stream	80.9%	18.0%	1.1%	100.0%
	MBBS	Count	164_a	28_a	1_a	193
		% within Stream	85.0%	14.5%	0.5%	100.0%
Total		Count	562	96	6	664
		% within Stream	84.6%	14.5%	0.9%	100.0%

Present study shows that overall 0.9% students were felling Dangerously sleepy, with highest amongst Physiotherapy students

Table No: 52. Stream V/S Berlin questionnaire for OSA

			BQ		Total
			No	Yes	
Stream	BPT	Count	136_a	4_a	140
		% within Stream	97.1%	2.9%	100.0%
	BHMS	Count	147_a	6_a	153
		% within Stream	96.1%	3.9%	100.0%
	Nursing	Count	175_a	3_a	178
		% within Stream	98.3%	1.7%	100.0%
	MBBS	Count	190_a	3_a	193
		% within Stream	98.4%	1.6%	100.0%
Total		Count	648	16	664
		% within Stream	97.6%	2.4%	100.0%

Out of total 2.4% positive students for OSA, highest positivity were seen in Homeopathy stream but contrary to it poor sleep quality was observed in physiotherapy students (Table 53)

Table No : 53. Stream V/S PSQI (Sleep Quality)

			PSQI		Total
			Good sleep quality	Poor sleep quality	
Stream	BPT	Count	114_a	26_b	140
		% within Stream	81.4%	18.6%	100.0%
	BHMS	Count	132_a	21_a	153
		% within Stream	86.3%	13.7%	100.0%
	Nursing	Count	170_a	8_b	178
		% within Stream	95.5%	4.5%	100.0%
	MBBS	Count	178_a	15_a	193
		% within Stream	92.2%	7.8%	100.0%
Total		Count	594	70	664
		% within Stream	89.5%	10.5%	100.0%

Table No: 54. Stream V/S PSQIDURAT (Duration of Sleep)

			PSQIDURAT				Total
			DURATION OF SLEEP >7 Hr	DURATION OF SLEEP < 7 and > 6	DURATION OF SLEEP < 6 and > 5	DURATION OF SLEEP <5 Hr	
Stream	BPT	Count	78_a	40_b	17_b	5_c	140
		% within Stream	55.7%	28.6%	12.1%	3.6%	100.0%
	BHMS	Count	142_a	9_b	2_b	$0_{a,b}$	153
		% within Stream	92.8%	5.9%	1.3%	0.0%	100.0%
	Nursing	Count	123_a	42_b	$13_{a,b}$	$0_{a,b}$	178
		% within Stream	69.1%	23.6%	7.3%	0.0%	100.0%
	MBBS	Count	169_a	19_b	5_b	$0_{a,b}$	193
		% within Stream	87.6%	9.8%	2.6%	0.0%	100.0%
Total		Count	512	110	37	5	664
		% within Stream	77.1%	16.6%	5.6%	0.8%	100.0%

Highest sleep disturbance was though it was only 2.1%, was observed in BPT students. Contrast to this observation, sleep latancy of more than one hour was observed only in MBBS students.

Table No : 55. Stream V/S PSQIDISTB (Sleep Disturbance)

			PSQIDISTB				
			No SLEEP DISTURBANCE	Little SLEEP DISTURBANCE	More SLEEP DISTURBANCE	Excessive SLEEP DISTURBANCE	T
Stream	BPT	Count	13_a	$99_{a, b}$	25_b	3_c	1
		% within Stream	9.3%	70.7%	17.9%	2.1%	10(
	BHMS	Count	19_a	105_a	29_a	0_a	1
		% within Stream	12.4%	68.6%	19.0%	0.0%	10(
	Nursing	Count	18_a	124_a	36_b	$0_{a, b}$	1
		% within Stream	10.1%	69.7%	20.2%	0.0%	10(
	MBBS	Count	47_a	138_b	8_c	$0_{a, b, c}$	1
		% within Stream	24.4%	71.5%	4.1%	0.0%	10(
Total		Count	97	466	98	3	6
		% within Stream	14.6%	70.2%	14.8%	0.5%	10(

Out of all four stream highest 41.5% participants from MBBS showed Better sleep Quality and was lowest amongst BPT students, with surprisingly 3-4 times a week medication use for getting sleep was observed in more than 3% cases. There was also highest dysfunctions in day to day life was observed in BPT Students. This all sought further investigation to find out to root cause of the problem prevailing amongst BPT Students

Table No : 56. Stream V/S PSQILATEN (Sleep Latency)

			PSQILATEN				
			Sleep Latency > 0 and < 15 min	Sleep Latency > 15 and < 30 min	Sleep Latency > 30 and < 60 min	Sleep Latency > 60 min	Total
Stream	BPT	Count	59_a	66_b	15_c	$0_{a, b, c}$	140
		% within Stream	42.1%	47.1%	10.7%	0.0%	100.0%
	BHMS	Count	56_a	$74_{a, b}$	23_b	$0_{a, b}$	153
		% within Stream	36.6%	48.4%	15.0%	0.0%	100.0%
	Nursing	Count	46_a	107_b	25_a	$0_{a, b}$	178
		% within Stream	25.8%	60.1%	14.0%	0.0%	100.0%
	MBBS	Count	34_a	84_b	69_c	6_d	193
		% within Stream	17.6%	43.5%	35.8%	3.1%	100.0%
Total		Count	195	331	132	6	664
		% within Stream	29.4%	49.8%	19.9%	0.9%	100.0%

Sleep latency was lowest amongst MBBS students and was highest among physiotherapy students and sleep latency of more than 60 minute was found in MBBS students only

Table No : 57. Stream V/S PSQISLPQUAL (Sleep Quality)

			PSQISLPQUAL				
			Better SLEEP QUALITY	Good SLEEP QUALITY	Poor SLEEP QUALITY	Worst SLEEP QUALITY	T
Stream	BPT	Count	34_a	$83_{a, b}$	17_b	6_b	1
		% within Stream	24.3%	59.3%	12.1%	4.3%	100
	BHMS	Count	47_a	92_a	11_a	3_a	1
		% within Stream	30.7%	60.1%	7.2%	2.0%	100
	Nursing	Count	48_a	112_a	16_a	2_a	1
		% within Stream	27.0%	62.9%	9.0%	1.1%	100
	MBBS	Count	80_a	100_b	9_b	$4_{a, b}$	1
		% within Stream	41.5%	51.8%	4.7%	2.1%	100
Total		Count	209	387	53	15	6
		% within Stream	31.5%	58.3%	8.0%	2.3%	100

Better sleep quality was amongst MBBS Students (41.5%), which was least in physiotherapy students. Overall 2.3% students were having worst sleep Quality

Table No : 58. Stream V/S PSQIMEDS (use of Medicine)

			No Medicine during the past month	less than once Medicine during the past week	once or twice Medicine during the past week	three to four times Medicine during the past week	Total
					PSQIMEDS		
Stream	BPT	Count	130_a	3_a	$2_{a, b}$	5_b	140
		% within Stream	92.9%	2.1%	1.4%	3.6%	100.0%
	BHMS	Count	148_a	3_a	1_a	1_a	153
		% within Stream	96.7%	2.0%	0.7%	0.7%	100.0%
	Nursing	Count	174_a	4_a	0_a	0_a	178
		% within Stream	97.8%	2.2%	0.0%	0.0%	100.0%
	MBBS	Count	$189_{a, b}$	$1_{a, b}$	3_b	0_a	193
		% within Stream	97.9%	0.5%	1.6%	0.0%	100.0%
Total		Count	641	11	6	6	664
		% within Stream	96.5%	1.7%	0.9%	0.9%	100.0%

It was good to note that 96.5% does not require medicine to get enough sleep

Table No : 59. Stream V/S PSQIDAYS (Dysfunction due to sleepiness)

			PSQIDAYS				
			DYSFUNCTION DUE TO SLEEPINESS : 0 DAY	DYSFUNCTION DUE TO SLEEPINESS : > 1 and < 2 DAY	DYSFUNCTION DUE TO SLEEPINESS : > 3 and < 4 DAY	DYSFUNCTION DUE TO SLEEPINESS : > 5 and < 6 DAY	T
Stream	BPT	Count	45_a	$80_{a, b}$	13_c	$2_{b, c}$	1
		% within Stream	32.1%	57.1%	9.3%	1.4%	10(
	BHMS	Count	62_a	79_a	11_a	1_a	1
		% within Stream	40.5%	51.6%	7.2%	0.7%	10(
	Nursing	Count	75_a	100_a	3_b	$0_{a, b}$	1
		% within Stream	42.1%	56.2%	1.7%	0.0%	10(
	MBBS	Count	93_a	97_a	3_b	$0_{a, b}$	1
		% within Stream	48.2%	50.3%	1.6%	0.0%	10(
Total		Count	275	356	30	3	6
		% within Stream	41.4%	53.6%	4.5%	0.5%	10(

Contrast to other indicator of poor sleep less than 65% of sleep efficiency was observed in nursing students while it was nil in medical students.

Table No : 60. Stream V/S PSQIHSE (SLEEP EFFICIENCY)

			PSQIHSE				Total
			SLEEP EFFICIENCY Y > 85	SLEEP EFFICIENCY Y < 85 and > 75,	SLEEP EFFICIENCY Y < 75 and > 65,	SLEEP EFFICIENCY Y < 65,	
Stream	BPT	Count	131_a	5_a	3_a	1_a	140
		% within Stream	93.6%	3.6%	2.1%	0.7%	100.0%
	BHMS	Count	139_a	8_a	4_a	2_a	153
		% within Stream	90.8%	5.2%	2.6%	1.3%	100.0%
	Nursing	Count	159_a	12_a	3_a	4_a	178
		% within Stream	89.3%	6.7%	1.7%	2.2%	100.0%
	MBBS	Count	185_a	6_a	2_a	0_a	193
		% within Stream	95.9%	3.1%	1.0%	0.0%	100.0%
Total		Count	614	31	12	7	664
		% within Stream	92.5%	4.7%	1.8%	1.1%	100.0%

Table No : 61. BMI V/S EPSS (Day time Sleepiness)

			EP			To
			Most likely getting enough sleep	May be suffering from excessive daytime sleepiness	Dangerously sleepy	
BMI	Overweight	Count	464_a	79_a	4_a	54
		% within BMI	84.8%	14.4%	0.7%	100.
	Pre Obese	Count	52_a	8_a	1_a	6
		% within BMI	85.2%	13.1%	1.6%	100.
	Obesity Grade 1	Count	35_a	6_a	1_a	4
		% within BMI	83.3%	14.3%	2.4%	100.
	Obesity Grade 2	Count	11_a	3_a	0_a	1
		% within BMI	78.6%	21.4%	0.0%	100.
Total		Count	562	96	6	66
		% within BMI	84.6%	14.5%	0.9%	100.

Obesity contributes significant to excessive daytime sleepiness of patients independently of sleep-disordered breathing. As a result, the provision of weight-loss promoting measures and close links to a dietician in a sleep disorders centre will be required to improve long term health outcomes. Presence of excessive daytime sleepiness, as measured by the ESS, was common in obese subjects but was not related to the presence or severity of OSA or other polysomnography findings in a selected group. It was related to older age, male gender, smoking, type 2 diabetes, symptoms of depression, and poor quality of life. It was also strongly associated with symptoms of disturbed nocturnal sleep. Excessive daytime sleepiness and obstructive sleep apnea are common disorders in obese subjects but seem to be largely unrelated in our study.

Table No : 62. BMI V/S BQ (Berlin Questioner)

			BQ		Total
			No	Yes	
BMI	Overweight	Count	540_a	7_b	547
		% within BMI	98.7%	1.3%	100.0%
	Pre Obese	Count	61_a	0_a	61
		% within BMI	100.0%	0.0%	100.0%
	Obesity Grade 1	Count	38_a	4_b	42
		% within BMI	90.5%	9.5%	100.0%
	Obesity Grade 2	Count	9_a	5_b	14
		% within BMI	64.3%	35.7%	100.0%
Total		Count	648	16	664
		% within BMI	97.6%	2.4%	100.0%

The prevalence of OSA in obese or severely obese patients is huge compare to normal weight adults. Furthermore, patients with mild OSA who gain 10% of their baseline weight are at a six fold-increased risk of progression of OSA, and an equivalent weight loss can result in a more than 20% improvement in OSA severity[118] Body mass index (BMI) has been widely accepted as a simple and the most practical measure of fatness in clinical and epidemiological surveys, even though it doesn't distinguish fat from lean body mass[119].

Obesity is recognized as an independent factor for the development of the cardiovascular diseases. Obesity implies increased body weight due to the enlargement of the adipose tissue to the extent that impairs health[120]. Abdominal (central) obesity is associated with dyslipidemia, impaired fasting glucose, insulin resistance and hypertension, which result in increased risk of cardio- and cerebrovascular diseases[121].

strong correlation between the central (abdominal) type of obesity and the cardiovascular and metabolic diseases and therefore sagittal abdominal diameter is shown to be a valid measurement of the visceral fat mass and cardio metabolic risk level sagittal abdominal diameter and neck length has shown a strong positive correlation with modified berlin questionnaire and may also be considered as a novel risk factor along with other gold standard anthropometric measurements like body mass index (BMI), waist-hip ratio (WHR) and neck circumference (NC) for diagnosis of OSA. In a resourse limited settings like ours, we can use ESS score alongwith BMI and NC for predicting patients who have very high probability of having OSA and these patients should undergo simple overnight oximetry study to diagnose OSA.

Table No : 63. BMI V/S PSQI (Good Sleep Quality)

			PSQI		Total
			Good sleep quality	Poor sleep quality	
BMI	Overweight	Count	490_a	57_a	547
		% within BMI	89.6%	10.4%	100.0%
	Pre Obese	Count	55_a	6_a	61
		% within BMI	90.2%	9.8%	100.0%
	Obesity Grade 1	Count	38_a	4_a	42
		% within BMI	90.5%	9.5%	100.0%
	Obesity Grade 2	Count	11_a	3_a	14
		% within BMI	78.6%	21.4%	100.0%
Total		Count	594	70	664
		% within BMI	89.5%	10.5%	100.0%

Based on response on PSQI there 10% difference in sleep quality percentage between overweight and obesity grade 2 participants, with as large as 21.4% students having poor sleep quality. Duration of sleep in hours more than 7 hours was seen in 512 participants while only 5 participates (0.8%) having less than 5 hours sleep

Table No : 64. BMI V/S PSQILATEN (Sleep Latency)

			PSQILATEN				
			Sleep Latency > 0 and < 15 min	Sleep Latency > 15 and < 30 min	Sleep Latency > 30 and < 60 min	Sleep Latency > 60 min	Total
BMI	Over weight	Count	164_a	265_a	112_a	6_a	547
		% within BMI	30.0%	48.4%	20.5%	1.1%	100.0
	Pre	Count	14_a	33_a	14_a	0_a	61

Obese	% within BMI	23.0%	54.1%	23.0%	0.0%	
Obesity Grade 1	Count	11_a	26_a	5_a	0_a	
	% within BMI	26.2%	61.9%	11.9%	0.0%	
Obesity Grade 2	Count	6_a	7_a	1_a	0_a	
	% within BMI	42.9%	50.0%	7.1%	0.0%	
Total	Count	195	331	132	0.9%	
	% within BMI	29.4%	49.8%	19.9%	6	

Sleep latency between 30 to 60 minutes were seen in 23% participants from obese category. And less than 15 minutes were in 42.9% participants from obesity grade 1

Table No : 65. BMI V/S PSQIHSE (Sleep Efficiency)

			PSQIHSE				
			SLEEP EFFICIENCY > 85	SLEEP EFFICIENCY < 85 and > 75,	SLEEP EFFICIENCY < 75 and > 65,	SLEEP EFFICIENCY < 65,	T
BMI	Over weight	Count	504_a	26_a	11_a	6_a	
		% within BMI	92.1%	4.8%	2.0%	1.1%	1(
	Pre Obese	Count	57_a	2_a	1_a	1_a	
		% within BMI	93.4%	3.3%	1.6%	1.6%	1(
	Obesity Grade 1	Count	39_a	3_a	0_a	0_a	
		% within BMI	92.9%	7.1%	0.0%	0.0%	1(

Obesity Grade 2	Count	14_a	0_a	0_a	0_a	14
	% within BMI	100.0%	0.0%	0.0%	0.0%	100.0%
Total	Count	614	31	12	7	664
	% within BMI	92.5%	4.7%	1.8%	1.1%	100.0%

The current study is in agreement with the Roane et al[122]. studies suggesting the future research should be studied in depth with the roles of sleep duration, sleep timing, and sleep variability and gender in weight gain (obesity). Sleep behaviors may be underlying, modifiable mechanisms that promote weight gain in different ways for men and women. Thus, more rigorous exploration into the independent, additive, and moderating roles of these modifiable mechanisms would provide valuable information to develop practical interventions for reducing weight gain, and potentially, obesity rates. The limitations of current study could be the neglecting nutritional details and we could have measure the hypertension in the medical students and this could fulfill in the future studies from our sample population. Our study concludes, sleep disturbance has affected the weight gain and the maximum number of subjects was lying down after the lunch and sitting and reading will be prone to develop obesity in future.

We found reduced vigilance in the context of poor sleep quality for severely obese individuals, but not individuals who were normal weight or overweight. Such findings highlight the possibility that severe obesity may confer a particular risk of decrements in attention with poor sleep quality.

Summary

In Present study was conducted at department of physiology to find out the sleep pattern of university students. we have studied total 664 participants, with highest 36.3% subject with age of 18-19, Amongst participants there were 34.3% Male and 65.7% Female. 23% BHMS, 21.1% BPT, 29.1% MBBS, 26.8% Nursing students. Average height of the participates were 159.17 ± 12.32 cm. Average weight of the participates were 54.25 ± 9.75 Kg. Average BMI of the participates were 21.7 ± 5.0 kg/m^2

In respect to **Epworth Calculator high chance of dozing was observed during** Lying down to rest in the afternoon (when possible) followed by Sitting quietly after lunch (not having had alcohol). 76.7 responses had total score of less than 10 in ESS result who are most likely getting enough sleep. 22.3 responses had total score between 10 to 15 in ESS result who may be suffering from enough day time sleepiness. 1response had total score of more tha 16 in ESS result who are dangerously sleepy.

In respect to **The Pittsburgh Sleep Quality Index** usual time of going to bed is 23.44 ± 1.72 PM with latency of 20.48 ± 15.44 Min. usual wake up time is 7.19 ± 1.55 AM and actual sleep they get at night is hours 7.53 ± 1.29. Good Quality of sleep was seen in 594 people with scores less than or equal to 5 while 70 people had scores more than 5 suggesting poor sleep Quality. In respect to

From **Berlin Questionnaire** we came to know that out of all only 3.6% participants are aware that they snoring. With Slightly louder than breathing in 34.2% cases, 0.6% had as loud as talking and 64.87% had Louder than talking Noise. Depending on frequency of snoring 4.4% had snoring 1-2 times/week, 0.9 % people snoring 3-4 times week and 0.8 % had snoring nearly every day. Out of all in 2.1% says that their snoring affect neighbor people nearly every day, in 45.9% case it happens 3-4 times and wk and in 51.7% cases it happens 1-2 times a week.

Out of all participants 8.9% feels tired or fatigue after sleep every day, 6.2 % feel it 3-4 times a week, 35.1% feels it 1-2 times in week and 35.1% never feels so. During waking time, Out of all 8.1% felts tired, fatigued or not up to par daily, 6.9% felt it 3-4 times a week, 36.6 % felt it 1-2 times a week and 48.2% never experience it. Only 2.0% responded that they nodded off or fallen asleep during driving vehicle.

Overall berlin score was positive in 2.4% cases suggestive of need of medical intervention and consultation with sleep expert . Detailed History of total 19 Subjects (16 with Positive BQ and 3 With ESS and PSQI Positive) was done after decoding of response was taken one to one and out of which one subject was found positive, thus Polysomnography Was done for that subject suggestive of high AHI index and advised medical intgervention

Conclusion

University students are very casual regarding their sleep habit, 28 students has Moderate Excessive Daytime Sleepiness, 6   students has Severe Excessive Daytime Sleepiness, 159 students have poor sleep quality, While high- risk for OSA was seen in 16 cases out of which, 1% of student suffer from OSA in present study. Contrasts to normal belief BPT student were having poor sleep hygiene compare to other streams. Appropriate measures and sleep hygiene education should therefore be emphasised in order to increase university student awareness on the importance of adopting healthy sleep hygiene practices. This is must to avoid consequences of sleep deprivation.

Limitations

&

Recommendations

The data used in this study were obtained from respondents in a health professional courses of **MKB** university and were recruited by convenience sampling, thus limiting the internal validity of the findings.

Moreover, they were generated via self-report, so they might not accurately reflect sleep habits or the nature of the difficulties students were actually experiencing.

Moreover, it was not possible to examine other factors affecting sleep such as alertness-promoting behaviors such as caffeine and nicotine use, living conditions e.g. overcrowded homes, sharing the bed with other siblings, TV viewing, and perceived education stress.

Inclusion of these factors could have resulted in a lengthy questionnaire that could have desisted people from filling all the details accurately due to boredom. Clearly, these are areas for further study, especially in Indian population.

Further studies are therefore suggested to compare the sleep hygiene practices and sleep quality of university students during school days and nonschool days, as well as between hostel residents and non-residential students.

References

Annexure

1. Thomas Dekker - Sleep is that golden chain that ties... [Internet]. [cited 2019 May 31]. Available from: https://www.brainyquote.com/quotes/thomas_dekker_204715

2. Wolfson AR, Carskadon MA. Sleep Schedules and Daytime Functioning in Adolescents. Child Dev [Internet]. 1998 Aug [cited 2019 Apr 19];69(4):875–87. Available from: http://doi.wiley.com/10.1111/j.1467-8624.1998.tb06149.x

3. Noland H, Price JH, Dake J, Telljohann SK. Adolescents' sleep behaviors and perceptions of sleep. J Sch Health. 2009;

4. Brown F, Soper B, Journal WBJ-CS, 2001 undefined. Prevalence of delayed sleep phase syndrome in university students. go.galegroup.com [Internet]. [cited 2018 Feb 15]; Available from: http://go.galegroup.com/ps/i.do?id=GALE%7CA80744660&sid=googleScholar&v=2.1&it=r&linkaccess=fulltext&issn=01463934&p=AONE&sw=w

5. Mesquita G, Reimão R. Effects of nighttime computer and television use. Arq Neuropsiquiatr. 2010;68(5):720–5.

6. sleep_and_teens_report1. o.galegroup.com [Internet]. [cited 2018 Feb 15]; Available from: http://go.galegroup.com/ps/i.do?id=GALE%7CA80744660&sid=googleScholar&v=2.1&it=r&linkaccess=fulltext&issn=01463934&p=AONE&sw=w

7. Kalra S, Bagnasco M, Otukonyong E, peptides MD-R, 2003 undefined. Rhythmic, reciprocal ghrelin and leptin signaling: new insight in the development of obesity. Elsevier [Internet]. [cited 2019 May 31]; Available from: https://www.sciencedirect.com/science/article/pii/S0167011502003051

8. Spiegel K, Tasali E, ... PP-A of internal, 2004 undefined. Brief communication: sleep curtailment in healthy young men is associated with decreased leptin levels, elevated ghrelin levels, and increased hunger and appetite. Am Coll Physicians [Internet]. [cited 2019 May 31]; Available from: http://annals.org/data/journals/aim/20078/0000605-200412070-00008.pdf

9. O 'brien EM, Mindell JA. Sleep and Risk-Taking Behavior in Adolescents. o.galegroup.com [Internet]. [cited 2018 Feb 15]; Available from: http://go.galegroup.com/ps/i.do?id=GALE%7CA80744660&sid=googleScholar&v=2.1&it=r&linkaccess=fulltext&issn=01463934&p=AONE&sw=w

10. Lancee J, van den Bout J, van Straten A, Spoormaker VI. Internet-delivered or mailed self-help treatment for insomnia? A randomized waiting-list controlled trial. Behav Res Ther. 2012;

11. Lack LC. Delayed Sleep and Sleep Loss in University Students. J Am Coll Heal [Internet]. 1986 Nov [cited 2018 Feb 15];35(3):105–10. Available from: http://www.tandfonline.com/doi/abs/10.1080/07448481.1986.9938970

12. Neuroscience SC-IJ of, 1994 undefined. The prevalence of self-reported sleep disturbances in young adults. Taylor Fr [Internet]. [cited 2018 Feb 15]; Available from: http://www.tandfonline.com/doi/abs/10.3109/00207459408986068

13. Buboltz WC, Brown F, Soper B. Sleep Habits and Patterns of College Students: A Preliminary Study. J Am Coll Heal [Internet]. 2001 Nov [cited 2018 Feb 15];50(3):131–5. Available from: http://www.tandfonline.com/doi/abs/1 0.1080/07448480109596017

14. Hicks R, Fernandez C. Striking changes in the sleep satisfaction of university students over the last two decades. Percept Mot [Internet]. 2001 [cited 2017 May 14]; Available from: http://pms.sagepub.com/content/93/3/660.short

15. Buysse D, Reynolds C, Monk T, Berman S. The Pittsburgh Sleep Quality Index: a new instrument for psychiatric practice and research. Psychiatry [Internet]. 1989 [cited 2017 May 14]; Available from: http://www.sciencedirect.com/science/article/pii/0165178189900474

16. Pilcher J, Ott E. The relationships between sleep and measures of health and weil-being in college students: A repeated measures approach. Behav Med [Internet]. 1998 [cited 2017 May 13]; Available from: http://www.tandfonline.com/doi/abs/10.1080/08964289809596373

17. Jean-Louis G, Kripke DF, Cole RJ, Assmus JD, Langer RD. Sleep detection with an accelerometer actigraph: Comparisons with polysomnography. Physiol Behav. 2001;

18. Taub JM, Hawkins DR. Aspects of personality associated with irregular sleep habits in young adults. J Clin Psychol [Internet]. 1979 Apr [cited 2018 Feb 15];35(2):296–304. Available from: http://doi.wiley.com/10.1002/1097- 4679%28197904%2935%n3A2 %3C296%3A%3AAID-JCLP2270350214%3E3.0.CO%3B2-X

19. Taub J, medicine RB-P, 1974 undefined. Acute shifts in the sleep-wakefulness cycle: Effects on performance and mood. psycnet.apa.org [Internet]. [cited 2018 Feb 15]; Available from: http://psycnet.apa.org/record/1975-00293-001

20. behavior JT-P&, 1980 undefined. Effects of ad lib extended-delayed sleep on

sensorimotor performance, memory and sleepiness in the young adult. Elsevier [Internet]. [cited 2018 Feb 15]; Available from: https://www.sciencedirect.com/science/article/pii/0031938480901857

21. Cofer L, Grice J, Sethre-Hofstad L, ... CR-H, 1999 undefined. Developmental perspectives on morningness-eveningness and social interactions. karger.com [Internet]. [cited 2018 Feb 15]; Available from: https://www.karger.com/Article/Abstract/22623

22. Machado ERS, Varella VBR, Andrade MMM. The Influence of Study Schedules and Work on the Sleep–Wake Cycle of College Students. Biol Rhythm Res [Internet]. 1998 Dec 9 [cited 2018 Feb 15];29(5):578–84. Available from: http://www.tandfonline.com/doi/abs/10.1076 /brhm.29.5.578.4827

23. Curcio G, Ferrara M, De Gennaro L. Sleep loss, learning capacity and academic performance. Sleep Medicine Reviews. 2006.

24. Review P, Online A, Module T, Id P, June P, El-Matbouly MA, et al. Clinical management of nocturnal enuresis. Pediatr Nephrol [Internet]. 2017 Aug 21 [cited 2017 Sep 5];12(8):1–12. Available from: http://linkinghub.elsevier.com/retrieve/pii /S1054139X17302574

25. Carskadon M, ... WD sleep, 2005 undefined. Normal human sleep: an overview. apsychoserver.psych.arizona.edu [Internet]. [cited 2019 May 31]; Available from: http://apsychoserver.psych.arizona.edu/jjbareprints/psyc501a/readings/Carskadon Dement 2011.pdf

26. Smith C. Sleep states and memory processes. Behav Brain Res [Internet]. 1995 [cited 2017 May 14]; Available from: http://www.sciencedirect.com/science/art icle/pii/016643289500024N

27. Young J, Bourgeois J, Hilty D. Sleep in hospitalized medical patients, part 1: factors affecting sleep. J Hosp [Internet]. 2008 [cited 2017 May 14]; Available from: http://onlinelibrary.wiley.com/doi/10.1002/jhm.372/full

28. Yang C, Wu C, Hsieh M, Liu M, Lu F. Coping with sleep disturbances among young adults: a survey of first-year college students in Taiwan. Behav Med [Internet]. 2003 [cited 2017 May 14]; Available from: http://www.tandfonline.com/doi/abs/10.1080/08964280309596066

29. Pagel J, Forister N, Kwiatkowki C. Adolescent sleep disturbance and school performance: the confounding variable of socioeconomics. J Clin sleep [Internet]. 2007 [cited 2017 May 14]; Available from:

http://europepmc.org/abstract/med/17557448

30. Cummings P, Koepsell T, Moffat J. Drowsiness, counter-measures to drowsiness, and the risk of a motor vehicle crash. Injury [Internet]. 2001 [cited 2017 May 14]; Available from: http://injuryprevention.bmj.com/content/7/3/194.short

31. Cole JB, Moore JC, Dolan BJ, O'Brien-Lambert A, Fryza BJ, Miner JR, et al. A Prospective Observational Study of Patients Receiving Intravenous and Intramuscular Olanzapine in the Emergency Department. Ann Emerg Med [Internet]. 2016 Nov [cited 2016 Nov 10]; Available from: http://linkinghub.elsevier.com/retrieve/pii/S0196064416304668

32. Carney CE, Edinger JD, Meyer B, Lindman L, Istre T. Daily activities and sleep quality in college students Is daily routine important for sleep? An Investigation of social rhythms in a clinical insomnia population. 2006;23(310):623–37.

33. Smaldone A, Honig J, Byrne M. Sleepless in America: inadequate sleep and relationships to health and well-being of our nation's children. Pediatrics [Internet]. 2007 [cited 2017 May 14]; Available from: http://pediatrics.aappublications.org/content/119/Supplement_1/S29.short

34. Breslau N, Roth T, Rosenthal L. Daytime sleepiness: an epidemiological study of young adults. Am J [Internet]. 1997 [cited 2017 May 14]; Available from: http://ajph.aphapublications.org/doi/abs/10.2105/AJPH.87.10.1649

35. Roth T, Ancoli-Israel S. Daytime consequences and correlates of insomnia in the United States: results of the 1991 National Sleep Foundation Survey. II. Sleep J Sleep Res Sleep [Internet]. 1999 [cited 2017 May 14]; Available from: http://psycnet.apa.org/psycinfo/1999-03090-001

36. Ban D, Lee T. Sleep duration, subjective sleep disturbances and associated factors among university students in Korea. J Korean Med Sci [Internet]. 2001 [cited 2017 May 14]; Available from: https://synapse.koreamed.org/pdf/10.3346/jkms.2001.16.4.475

37. Belísio[1] AS, Louzada[2] FM, Virginia C, De Azevedo[1] M. Influence of social factors on the sleep-wake cycle in children.

38. Gaultney JF. The Prevalence of Sleep Disorders in College Students: Impact on Academic Performance. J Am Coll Heal [Internet]. 2010;59(2):91–7. Available from: http://www.tandfonline.com/loi/vach20

39. Wali S, Krayem A, Samman Y, Mirdad S. Sleep disorders in Saudi health care workers. Ann Saudi [Internet]. 1998 [cited 2017 May 14]; Available from:

http://europepmc.org/abstract/med/17277504

40. BaHammam A, Saeed A Bin, Al-Faris E. Sleep duration and its correlates in a sample of Saudi elementary school children. Singapore Med [Internet]. 2006 [cited 2017 May 14]; Available from: http://www.smj.org.sg/sites/default/files/4710/4710a7.pdf

41. Biggeri L, Bini M, Grilli L. The transition from university to work: a multilevel approach to the analysis of the time to obtain the first job. R Stat Soc Ser ... [Internet]. 2001   [cited   2017   May   14];   Available   from: http://onlinelibrary.wiley.com/doi/10.1111/1467-985X.00203/full

42. Pilcher J, Ginter D, Sadowsky B. Sleep quality versus sleep quantity: relationships between sleep and measures of health, well-being and sleepiness in college students. J Psychosom Res [Internet]. 1997 [cited 2017 May 14]; Available from: http://www.sciencedirect.com/science/article/pii/S0022399997000044

43. Veasey S, Rosen R, Darzansky B, Rosen I, Owens J. Sleep loss and fatigue in residency training: a reappraisal. Jama [Internet]. 2002 [cited 2017 May 14]; Available from: http://jamanetwork.com/journals/jama/fullarticle/195255

44. Fletcher K, Underwood W, Davis S. Effects of work hour reduction on residents' lives: a systematic review. Jama [Internet]. 2005 [cited 2017 May 14]; Available from: http://jama.jamanetwork.com/article.aspx?articleid=201482

45. Greenfield LJ. Limiting resident duty hours. Am J Surg [Internet]. 2003 Jan;185(1):10–2.   Available   from: http://linkinghub.elsevier.com/retrieve/pii/S0002961002011443

46. Parthasarathy S. Sleep and the medical profession. Curr Opin Pulm Med [Internet]. 2005   Nov;11(6):507–12.   Available   from: http://www.ncbi.nlm.nih.gov/pubmed/16217176

47. Owens J, Veasey S, Rosen R. Physician, heal thyself: sleep, fatigue, and medical education. SLEEP-NEW YORK- [Internet]. 2001 [cited 2017 May 14]; Available from: https://www.researchgate.net/profile/Sigrid_Veasey/publication/11861707_Physician_ Heal_thyself_sleep_fatigue_and_medical_education/links/0c96052ebb7255ab5400000 0.pdf

48. Howard S, Gaba D, Rosekind M. The risks and implications of excessive daytime sleepiness in resident physicians. Academic [Internet]. 2002 [cited 2017 May 14]; Available   from: http://journals.lww.com/academicmedicine/Abstract/2002/10000/The_Risks_and_Impl

ications_of_Excessive_Daytime.15.aspx

49.   Anders T, Eiben L. Pediatric sleep disorders: a review of the past 10 years. J Am Acad Child [Internet]. 1997 [cited 2017 May 14]; Available from: http://www.sciencedirect.com/science/article/pii/S0890856709636947

50.   Lewis M. Child and adolescent psychiatry: A comprehensive textbook [Internet]. 2002 [cited 2017 May 14]. Available from: http://psycnet.apa.org/psycinfo/2003-00440-000

51.   Ohayon M, Roberts R, Zulley J, Smirne S. Prevalence and patterns of problematic sleep among older adolescents. J Am [Internet]. 2000 [cited 2017 May 14]; Available from: http://www.sciencedirect.com/science/article/pii/S089085670960424X

52.   Ağargün M, Kara H, Solmaz M. Subjective sleep quality and suicidality in patients with major depression. J Psychiatr Res [Internet]. 1997 [cited 2017 May 14]; Available from: http://www.sciencedirect.com/science/article/pii/S0022395696000374

53.   Lomelí HA, Pérez-Olmos I, Talero-Gutiérrez C, Moreno CB, González-Reyes R, Palacios L, et al. Sleep evaluation scales and questionnaires: A review. Actas Espanolas de Psiquiatria. 2008.

54.   Prinz P, Hertrich K, Hirschfelder U, de Zwaan M. Burnout, depression and depersonalisation--psychological factors and coping strategies in dental and medical students. GMS Z Med Ausbild. 2012;29(1):1–14.

55.   Sajatovic M, Ramirez L. Rating scales in mental health. 2nd eds. Ohio: Lexi Comp. 2003 [cited 2017 May 14]; Available from: https://scholar.google.co.in/scholar?q=Sajatovic+M.+Rating+Scales+in+Mental+Health%2C+2nd+ed.+Hudson%3A+Lexy-Comp+Inc.%2C+2003%3B+p.+9-21%2C+365-9.&btnG=&hl=en&as_sdt=0%2C5

56.   Martini J, Petzoldt J, Knappe S, Garthus-Niegel S, Asselmann E, Wittchen H-U. Infant, maternal, and familial predictors and correlates of regulatory problems in early infancy: The differential role of infant temperament and maternal anxiety and depression. Early Hum Dev [Internet]. 2017 Sep 1 [cited 2017 Sep 5];115:23–31. Available from: http://linkinghub.elsevier.com/retrieve/pii/S0378378217302244

57.   Anders T, & LE-J of the AA of C, 1997 undefined. Pediatric sleep disorders: a review of the past 10 years. Elsevier [Internet]. [cited 2018 Feb 16]; Available from: https://www.sciencedirect.com/science/article/pii/S0890856709636947

58.   Escobar-Córdoba F, Neurol JE-S-R, 2005 undefined. Validación colombiana del índice de calidad de sueño de Pittsburgh. researchgate.net [Internet]. [cited 2018 Feb 16]; Available from: https://www.researchgate.net/profile/Franklin_Escobar-

Cordoba/publication/269987211_Colombian_Validation_of_the_Pittsburgh_Sleep_Qu
ality_Index_Validacion_colombiana_del_indice_de_calidad_de_sueno_de_Pittsburgh/
links/545806970cf2bccc49111b57/Colombian-Validation-of-the-Pittsburgh-Sleep-
Quality-Index-Validacion-colombiana-del-indice-de-calidad-de-sueno-de-
Pittsburgh.pdf

59. Sadeh A. A brief screening questionnaire for infant sleep problems: validation and findings for an Internet sample. Pediatrics [Internet]. 2004 [cited 2017 May 14]; Available from: http://pediatrics.aappublications.org/content/113/6/e570.short

60. Bruni O, Ottaviano S, Guidetti V, Romoli M. The Sleep Disturbance Scale for Children (SDSC) Construct ion and validation of an instrument to evaluate sleep disturbances in childhood and adolescence. J sleep [Internet]. 1996 [cited 2017 May 14]; Available from: http://onlinelibrary.wiley.com/doi/10.1111/j.1365-2869.1996.00251.x/full

61. Chervin R, Hedger K, Dillon J, Pituch K. Pediatric sleep questionnaire (PSQ): validity and reliability of scales for sleep-disordered breathing, snoring, sleepiness, and behavioral problems. Sleep Med [Internet]. 2000 [cited 2017 May 14]; Available from: http://www.sciencedirect.com/science/article/pii/S138994579900009X

62. Morin C, Barlow D. Insomnia: Psychological assessment and management. 1993 [cited 2017 May 14]; Available from: https://scholar.google.co.in/scholar?q=Morin+C.+Insomnia%3A+psychological+asses sment+and+management.+New+York%2C+London%3A+The+Guilford+Press%2C+ 1993.+&btnG=&hl=en&as_sdt=0%2C5

63. Smith S, Trinder J. Detecting insomnia: comparison of four self-report measures of sleep in a young adult population. J Sleep Res [Internet]. 2001 [cited 2017 May 14]; Available from: http://onlinelibrary.wiley.com/doi/10.1046/j.1365-2869.2001.00262.x/full

64. Rosenthal L, Roehrs T, Roth T. The sleep-wake activity inventory: a self-report measure of daytime sleepiness. Biol Psychiatry [Internet]. 1993 [cited 2017 May 14]; Available from: http://www.sciencedirect.com/science/article/pii/000632239390070T

65. Greenland S, Stephen Senn BJ, Kenneth Rothman BJ, John Carlin BB, Charles Poole B, Steven Goodman BN, et al. Statistical tests, P values, confidence intervals, and power: a guide to misinterpretations. Eur J Epidemiol. 31.

66. Espie C, Inglis S, Harvey L, Tessier S. Insomniacs' attributions: psychometric properties of the dysfunctional beliefs and attitudes about sleep scale and the sleep

disturbance questionnaire. J Psychosom [Internet]. 2000 [cited 2017 May 14]; Available from: http://www.sciencedirect.com/science/article/pii/S0022399999000902

67.   Giannotti F, Cortesi F, Sebastiani T. Circadian preference, sleep and daytime behaviour in adolescence. J sleep [Internet]. 2002 [cited 2017 May 15]; Available from: http://onlinelibrary.wiley.com/doi/10.1046/j.1365-2869.2002.00302.x/full

68.   Thorleifsdottir B, Björnsson J, Benediktsdottir B. Sleep and sleep habits from childhood to young adulthood over a 10-year period. J [Internet]. 2002 [cited 2017 May 15]; Available from: http://www.sciencedirect.com/science/article/pii/S0022399902004440

69.   Webb W, Bonnet M, Blume G. A post-sleep inventory. Percept Mot Skills [Internet]. 1976 [cited 2017 May 15]; Available from: http://pms.sagepub.com/content/43/3/987.short

70.   Johns M, Gay T, Goodyear M. Sleep habits of healthy young adults: use of a sleep questionnaire. Br J [Internet]. 1971 [cited 2017 May 15]; Available from: http://jech.bmj.com/content/25/4/236.full.pdf

71.   Zammit G. Subjective ratings of the characteristics and sequelae of good and poor sleep in normals. J Clin Psychol [Internet]. 1988 [cited 2017 May 15]; Available from: http://onlinelibrary.wiley.com/doi/10.1002/1097-4679(198803)44:2%3C123::AID-JCLP2270440206%3E3.0.CO;2-D/full

72.   Carskadon M, Seifer R, Acebo C. Reliability of six scales in a sleep questionnaire for adolescents. Sleep Res [Internet]. 1991 [cited 2017 May 15]; Available from: https://scholar.google.co.in/scholar?q=Carskadon+MA%2C+Seifer+R%2C+Acebo+C. +Reliability+of+six+scales+in+a+sleep+questionnaire+for+adolescents.+Sleep+Res+1 991b%3B20%3A421.&btnG=&hl=en&as_sdt=0%2C5

73.   Carskadon M, Seifer R, Davis S, Acebo C. Sleep, sleepiness and mood in college-bound high school seniors. Sleep Res [Internet]. 1991 [cited 2017 May 15]; Available from: https://scholar.google.co.in/scholar?q=Carskadon+MA%2C+Seifer+R%2C+Davis+S %2C+Acebo+C.+Sleepiness+in+collegebound+high+school+seniors.+Sleep+Res+199 1a%3B20%3A175.+&btnG=&hl=en&as_sdt=0%2C5

74.   Parrott A, Hindmarch I. Factor analysis of a sleep evaluation questionnaire. Psychol Med [Internet]. 1978 [cited 2017 May 15]; Available from: http://journals.cambridge.org/article_S0033291700014379

75.   Åkerstedt T, Hume K, Minors D. The subjective meaning of good sleep, an

intraindividual approach using the Karolinska Sleep Diary. Mot Ski [Internet]. 1994 [cited 2017 May 15]; Available from: http://journals.sagepub.com/doi/abs/10.2466/pms.1994.79.1.287

76. Lindberg E, Elmasry A, Janson C. Reported snoring–does validity differ by age? sleep Res [Internet]. 2000 [cited 2017 May 27]; Available from: http://onlinelibrary.wiley.com/doi/10.1046/j.1365-2869.2000.00199.x/full

77. Soldatos C, Dikeos D, Paparrigopoulos T. Athens Insomnia Scale: validation of an instrument based on ICD-10 criteria. J Psychosom [Internet]. 2000 [cited 2017 May 27]; Available from: http://www.sciencedirect.com/science/article/pii/S0022399900000957

78. Jenkins C, Stanton B, Niemcryk S. A scale for the estimation of sleep problems in clinical research. J Clin [Internet]. 1988 [cited 2017 May 27]; Available from: http://www.sciencedirect.com/science/article/pii/0895435688901382

79. Douglass A, Bornstein R, Nino-Murcia G, Keenan S. Creation of the ASDC sleep disorders questionnaire. Sleep Res [Internet]. 1986 [cited 2017 May 27]; Available from: https://scholar.google.co.in/scholar?q=Douglass+AB%2C+Bornstein+R%2C+Nino-Murcia+G%2C+Keenan+S%2C+Milers+L%2C+Zarcone+VP.+Creation+of+the+ASDC+Sleep+Disorders+Questionnaire.+J+Sleep+Res+1986%3B15%3A117.+&btnG=&hl=en&as_sdt=0%2C5

80. Magnusson A, Friis S, affective SO-J of, 1997 undefined. Internal consistency of the seasonal pattern assessment questionnaire (SPAQ). jad-journal.com [Internet]. [cited 2018 Feb 18]; Available from: http://www.jad-journal.com/article/S0165-0327(96)00104-8/abstract

81. Shahid A, Wilkinson K, Marcu S, Shapiro CM. Leeds Sleep Evaluation Questionnaire (LSEQ). In: STOP, THAT and One Hundred Other Sleep Scales [Internet]. New York, NY: Springer New York; 2011 [cited 2018 Feb 19]. p. 211–3. Available from: http://link.springer.com/10.1007/978-1-4419-9893-4_48

82. Johns MW. A New Method for Measuring Daytime Sleepiness: The Epworth Sleepiness Scale. Sleep. 14(6):540–5.

83. Reynolds C, Monk T, Berman S, Kupfer D. The Pittsburgh Sleep Quality Index: a new instrument for psychiatric practice and research. Psychiatry Res [Internet]. 1989 [cited 2017 May 14]; Available from: http://www.w.esmotech.com/sites/default/files/Original-Pittsburgh-Sleep-Quality-Index-PSQI-paper-1988.pdf

84. Beaton S, Voge S. Measurements for long-term care: a guidebook for nurses. 1998 [cited 2017 May 14]; Available from: https://scholar.google.co.in/scholar?q=Beaton+SR%2C+Voge+SA.+Measurements+fo r+long- term+care%3A+a+guidebook+for+nurses.+ London%3A+SAGE+Publications%3B+1998&btnG=&hl=en&as_sdt=0%2C5

85. Netzer N, Stoohs R, Netzer C. Using the Berlin Questionnaire to identify patients at risk for the sleep apnea syndrome. Ann Intern [Internet]. 1999 [cited 2017 May 14]; Available from: http://annals.org/aim/article/712967/using-berlin-questionnaire- identify-patients-risk-sleep-apnea-syndrome

86. Lund H, Reider B, ... AW-J of adolescent, 2010 undefined. Sleep patterns and predictors of disturbed sleep in a large population of college students. Elsevier [Internet]. [cited 2019 Apr 19]; Available from: https://www.sciencedirect.com/science/article/pii/S1054139X09002389

87. Roenneberg T, Kantermann T, Juda M, clocks CV-C, 2013 undefined. Light and the human circadian clock. Springer [Internet]. [cited 2019 Apr 19]; Available from: https://link.springer.com/chapter/10.1007/978-3-642-25950-0_13

88. Pilcher J, Ginter D, research BS-J of psychosomatic, 1997 undefined. Sleep quality versus sleep quantity: relationships between sleep and measures of health, well-being and sleepiness in college students. Elsevier [Internet]. [cited 2018 Feb 15]; Available from: https://www.sciencedirect.com/science/article/pii/S0022399997000044

89. Health LL-J of AC, 1986 undefined. Delayed sleep and sleep loss in university students. Taylor Fr [Internet]. [cited 2019 Apr 19]; Available from: https://www.tandfonline.com/doi/abs/10.1080/07448481.1986.9938970

90. Hawkins J, Sleep PS-, 1992 undefined. Self-reported sleep quality in college students: a repeated measures approach. academic.oup.com [Internet]. [cited 2019 Apr 19]; Available from: https://academic.oup.com/sleep/article-abstract/15/6/545/2749320

91. Valdez P, Ramírez C, García A. Delaying and Extending Sleep During Weekends: Sleep Recovery or Circadian Effect? Chronobiol Int [Internet]. 1996 Jan 7 [cited 2019 Apr 19];13(3):191–8. Available from: http://www.tandfonline.com/doi/full/10.3109/07420529609012652

92. Hicks RA, Fernandez C, Pellegrini RJ. The Changing Sleep Habits of University Students: An Update. Percept Mot Skills [Internet]. 2001 Dec 31 [cited 2019 Apr 19];93(3):648–648. Available from: http://journals.sagepub.com/doi/10.2466/pms.2001.93.3.648

93.   Singleton RA, Wolfson AR. Alcohol Consumption, Sleep, and Academic Performance Among College Students. J Stud Alcohol Drugs [Internet]. 2009 May [cited 2019 Apr 19];70(3):355–63.   Available   from: http://www.jsad.com/doi/10.15288/jsad.2009.70.355

94.   Tsai L, research SL-J of psychosomatic, 2004 undefined. Sleep patterns in college students: Gender and grade differences. Elsevier [Internet]. [cited 2019 Apr 19]; Available   from: https://www.sciencedirect.com/science/article/pii/S0022399903005075

95.   Buboltz WC, Brown F, Soper B. Sleep Habits and Patterns of College Students: A Preliminary Study. J Am Coll Heal [Internet]. 2001 Nov [cited 2019 Apr 19];50(3):131–5.   Available   from: http://www.tandfonline.com/doi/abs/10.1080/07448480109596017

96   Ohayon M, Sleep RR , 2001 undefined. Comparability of Sleep Disorders Diagnoses Using DSM-IV and ICSD Classifications with Adolescents. academic.oup.com [Internet].   [cited   2019   Apr   19];   Available   from: https://academic.oup.com/sleep/article-abstract/24/8/920/2750042

97.   Ahn S-H, Kim Y-H, Shin C-H, Lee J-S, Kim B-J, Kim Y-J, et al. Cardiac Vulnerability to Cerebrogenic Stress as a Possible Cause of Troponin Elevation in Stroke. J Am Heart Assoc [Internet]. 2016 Oct 6 [cited 2016 Nov 10];5(10). Available from: http://www.ncbi.nlm.nih.gov/pubmed/27792642

98.   Gradisar M, Wolfson A, Harvey A, … LH-… of CS, 2013 undefined. The sleep and technology use of Americans: findings from the National Sleep Foundation's 2011 Sleep in America poll. jcsm.aasm.org [Internet]. [cited 2019 Apr 19]; Available from: http://jcsm.aasm.org/viewabstract.aspx?pid=29249&k_clickid=%2Fwellness%2F

99.   history EL-S disorders: natural, epidemiology undefined, 1983 undefined. Good and poor sleepers: an epidemiological survey of the San Marino population. ci.nii.ac.jp [Internet]. [cited 2019 Apr 20]; Available from: https://ci.nii.ac.jp/naid/10013257522/

100. Mellinger G, Balter M. Insomnia and its treatment: prevalence and correlates. Arch Gen   [Internet].   1985   [cited   2017   May   13];   Available   from: http://archpsyc.jamanetwork.com/article.aspx?articleid=493528

101. Karacan I, Thornby J, Anch M, … CH-SS&, 1976 undefined. Prevalence of sleep disturbance in a primarily urban Florida county. Elsevier [Internet]. [cited 2019 Apr 20];   Available   from: https://www.sciencedirect.com/science/article/pii/0037785676900068

102. McGhie A, Science SR-J of M, 1962 undefined. The subjective assessment of normal sleep patterns. cambridge.org [Internet]. [cited 2019 Apr 20]; Available from: https://www.cambridge.org/core/journals/journal-of-mental-science/article/subjective-assessment-of-normal-sleep-patterns/719DB54DB7B02A62FE0E0B2A78E18378

103. Kaur G. A Study on the Sleep Quality of Indian College Students. JSM Brain. 2018;3(1):1018.

104. Bliwise D, King A, Harris R, medicine WH-S science &, 1992 undefined. Prevalence of self-reported poor sleep in a healthy population aged 50–65. Elsevier [Internet]. [cited 2019 Apr 20]; Available from: https://www.sciencedirect.com/science/article/pii/027795369290066Y

105. Broman J, Lundh L, Neurophysiology JH-C, 1996 undefined. Insufficient sleep in the general population. Elsevier [Internet]. [cited 2019 Apr 20]; Available from: https://www.sciencedirect.com/science/article/pii/0987705396815322

106. Brown FC, Buboltz WC, Soper B. Relationship of Sleep Hygiene Awareness, Sleep Hygiene Practices, and Sleep Quality in University Students.

107. Talk About Sleep - Sleep for Health and Vitality [Internet]. [cited 2019 Jun 3]. Available from: https://www.talkaboutsleep.com/

108. Socioeconomic Status, Gender And Marital Status Influence Sleep Disturbances -- ScienceDaily [Internet]. [cited 2019 Jun 3]. Available from: https://www.sciencedaily.com/releases/2009/06/090610091331.htm

109. Zhang Z, Chen T, Ngming Jin X, Yan C, Shen X, Li S. Sleep Patterns, Sleep Problems and Associations with Reported Sleep Quality in Chinese School-Aged Children. Am J Public Heal Res [Internet]. 2013;1(4):93–100. Available from: http://pubs.sciepub.com/ajphr/1/4/3

110. Wilhoit S, Chest PS-, 1987 undefined. Obstructive sleep apnea in premenopausal women: a comparison with men and with postmenopausal women. Elsevier [Internet]. [cited 2019 Apr 20]; Available from: https://www.sciencedirect.com/science/article/pii/S0012369216587947

111. Sleep RA-, 1995 undefined. The distribution of EEG frequencies in REM and NREM sleep stages in healthy young adults. academic.oup.com [Internet]. [cited 2019 Apr 20]; Available from: https://academic.oup.com/sleep/article-abstract/18/5/334/2749667

112. BAKER FC, TURLINGTON SR, COLRAIN I. Developmental changes in the sleep electroencephalogram of adolescent boys and girls. J Sleep Res [Internet]. 2012 Feb [cited 2019 Apr 20];21(1):59–67. Available from:

http://doi.wiley.com/10.1111/j.1365-2869.2011.00930.x

113. Campbell I, Grimm K, ... EDB-P of the, 2012 undefined. Sex, puberty, and the timing of sleep EEG measured adolescent brain maturation. Natl Acad Sci [Internet]. [cited 2019 Apr 20]; Available from: https://www.pnas.org/content/109/15/5740.short

114. Carrier J, Viens I, Poirier G, Robillard R, Lafortune M, Vandewalle G, et al. Sleep slow wave changes during the middle years of life. Eur J Neurosci [Internet]. 2011 Feb [cited 2019 Apr 20];33(4):758–66. Available from: http://doi.wiley.com/10.1111/j.1460-9568.2010.07543.x

115. Feinberg I, cognition IC-B and, 2010 undefined. Sleep EEG changes during adolescence: an index of a fundamental brain reorganization. Elsevier [Internet]. [cited 2019 Apr 20]; Available from: https://www.sciencedirect.com/science/article/pii/S0278262609001791

116. Mourtazaev M, Kemp B, Sleep AZ, 1995 undefined. Age and gender affect different characteristics of slow waves in the sleep EEG. academic.oup.com [Internet]. [cited 2019 Apr 20]; Available from: https://academic.oup.com/sleep/article-abstract/18/7/557/2749691

117. Zhao L, Tan A, Tai B, Loo G, ... HT-J of CS, 2014 undefined. Effects of gender on the prevalence of obstructive sleep apnea in patients with coronary artery disease. jcsm.aasm.org [Internet]. [cited 2019 Apr 20]; Available from: http://jcsm.aasm.org/ViewAbstract.aspx?pid=29789

118. Peppard P, Young T, Palta M, Dempsey J, Jama JS-, 2000 undefined. Longitudinal study of moderate weight change and sleep-disordered breathing. jamanetwork.com [Internet]. [cited 2019 Apr 20]; Available from: https://jamanetwork.com/journals/jama/article-abstract/193382

119. Iribarren C, Sharp DS, Burchfiel CM, Petrovitch H. Association of Weight Loss and Weight Fluctuation with Mortality among Japanese American Men. N Engl J Med [Internet]. 1995 Sep 14 [cited 2019 Apr 20];333(11):686–92. Available from: http://www.nejm.org/doi/abs/10.1056/NEJM199509143331102

120. Stokić E, Srdić B, ... VB-RA in, 2012 undefined. Sagittal abdominal diameter as the anthropometric measure of cardiovascular risk. intechopen.com [Internet]. [cited 2019 Apr 20]; Available from: https://www.intechopen.com/download/pdf/32673

121. Siöström CD, Lissner L, Siostrom L. Relationships Between Changes in Body Composition and Changes in Cardiovascular Risk Factors: The SOS Intervention Study. Obes Res [Internet]. 1997 Nov [cited 2019 Apr 20];5(6):519–30. Available

from: http://doi.wiley.com/10.1002/j.1550-8528.1997.tb00572.x

122. Roane BM, Seifer R, Sharkey KM, Van Reen E, Bond TLY, Raffray T, et al. What Role Does Sleep Play in Weight Gain in the First Semester of University? Behav Sleep Med [Internet]. 2015 Nov 2 [cited 2019 Jun 5];13(6):491–505. Available from: http://www.ncbi.nlm.nih.gov/pubmed/25115969

CPSIA information can be obtained
at www.ICGtesting.com
Printed in the USA
LVHW080413301222
736096LV00030B/716